Also by James van Sweden

THE ARTFUL GARDEN

THE ARTFUL GARDEN

CREATIVE INSPIRATION
FOR LANDSCAPE DESIGN

James van Sweden

and TOM CHRISTOPHER

 RANDOM HOUSE / NEW YORK

Copyright © 2011 by James van Sweden

Published in the United States by Random House,
an imprint of The Random House Publishing Group,
a division of Random House, Inc., New York.

RANDOM HOUSE and colophon are
registered trademarks of Random House, Inc.

LIBRARY OF CONGRESS CATALOGING-IN-PUBLICATION DATA
van Sweden, James
The artful garden: creative inspiration
for landscape design/
by James van Sweden and Thomas Christopher.
p. cm.
ISBN 978-1-4000-6389-5
1. Gardens—Design. 2. Art and design.
I. Christopher, Thomas. II. Title.
SB472.45.V35 2011
712—dc22   2010029329

Printed in China

www.atrandom.com

9 8 7 6 5 4 3 2 1

FIRST EDITION

Book design by Barbara M. Bachman

For David and Perrin Lilly

CONTENTS

HELEN FRANKENTHALER, *NATURE ABHORS A VACUUM*, 1973. ACRYLIC
ON CANVAS. 103 1/2" X 112". PATRONS' PERMANENT FUND AND GIFT OF
AUDREY AND DAVID MIRVISH. Image courtesy of the National Gallery
of Art, Washington, D.C. © Helen Frankenthaler / Artists Rights Society
(ARS), New York.

INTRODUCTION

THE NEW ISLAND in Chicago Botanic Garden's Great Basin posed a stark contrast to the lush vegetation on every side— as yet, it was just five acres of spoil, earth, gravel, and rock dredged from the lake floor. But Pleasant Rowland, the creator of the American Girl doll, had donated funds to turn this barren expanse into an "evening garden," a sanctuary from which to enjoy the view west toward the sunset, and my firm was one of four invited to make a presentation to her and the jury. I had passed the previous afternoon here, watching the shadows lengthen and the sun drop toward the horizon. This would be a magnificent commission for any landscape architect, especially in terms of visibility—the Chicago Botanic Garden, one of the leading institutions of its kind in the United States, attracts almost a million visitors every year.

It was morning now. Sheila Brady, one of my partners at Oehme, van Sweden & Associates, was with me, and together we made some last-minute notes about the site's potential. In a few minutes, we'd be making our presentation. We'd have an hour to make our case, to share our vision. Our principal means for accomplishing that would be the twenty slides we had pulled from our files before leaving Washington, D.C. In selecting these we had concentrated, naturally, on photographs of gardens we had designed for public spaces. We'd devoted a lot of time and thought to those choices. What we wanted were definitive images, ones that epitomized our firm's style.

In the midst of the hunt I remembered a slide I had saved of a Helen Frankenthaler painting, a huge work (8' 7.5" by 9' 4.5") titled, appropriately, *Nature Abhors a Vacuum*. When I first saw this painting years ago, I was struck by the warm hues, so like the russets and golds of our firm's meadow-inspired landscapes. I loved the painting's energy, the way that masses of color sweep across the canvas, melting into one another where they intersect. This, the controlled sensuality and passion of the painting, seemed identical to what I aim for in my own design, and I had kept the slide as a sort of talisman. On a whim, I had slipped it into the carousel.

The time came for the presentation—our audition—and Sheila and I walked to the front of the conference room. As the senior member of the firm, I called for the lights to be dimmed, and the first slide flashed onto the screen. An hour later, almost the minute we finished speaking to the jury, I knew we had the job. Pleasant Rowland was the first person to approach; her manner was eager. She said that she couldn't believe I had shown a Helen Frankenthaler painting, that she was just crazy about Frankenthaler's work, that she had been riveted by that slide. Clearly, the painting had spoken to her more powerfully than words ever could. For a minute, with the Frankenthaler before us, she and I and, I suppose, everyone in that room had shared the same vision of the color, energy, and grace that could be that garden. They had actually seen and felt what as yet existed only in my mind.

A week later, we were notified that we had in fact gotten the commission. Amid the celebration at our offices, the germ of an idea occurred to me: the need for this book.

THE HYBRID ART

For me, the remarkable aspect of this incident was not that a painting should play the central role in the creation of a garden. What struck me as far more notable was the attitude of many other people involved in this project (though not Pleasant Rowland): that they were surprised by my use of another art form as part of the design process. Few of us, whether professional or amateur, would, if asked, deny that garden design is a fine art. Yet, with rare exceptions, we do not treat it as such. We take our inspiration from nursery catalogs or gardens that we have visited. Maybe we think it would be pretentious to compare what we do to what we might find on the wall of a gallery or on a pedestal in the Louvre. The truth is, though, by failing to make this connection, we rob ourselves of what should be the designer's most powerful tool and guide.

Don't get me wrong. I think it's essential to look at horticultural precedents. I love to talk plants with other gardeners, or spend a day just absorbing some well-crafted landscape. But I also know how important it is to keep in touch with a broader aesthetic world.

Influences and ideas flow back and forth between the other arts as a matter of course. Sculptors commonly step into painting for a while, using the sense of mass they have developed in the former medium to inform the latter. Likewise, the issues of color, surface, and line they explore in painting can continue to serve them when they switch back to working in three dimensions. Composers collaborate with choreographers and both learn from each other; a book inspires a movie or a movie inspires a play; themes and perspectives from the visual arts reemerge in poetry. What commonly results from this cross-fertilization is the artistic equivalent of the phenomenon that horticulturists call "hybrid vigor": the offspring of such a cross is bigger and bolder, more energized, than either of the parents.

Gardeners miss a lot by ignoring the work of those who are really their colleagues. I cannot, for instance, recall a single case of a client coming to me and telling me that they wanted their garden to have the detailed richness of a Vermeer or the rhythmic swing of Duke Ellington. As I get to know them, however (and the client-designer relationship must be a close one for the process to succeed), I commonly find that clients have a passionate devotion to other art forms, whether high art or popular or both. Indeed, I have learned to look for this, as it is in such enthusiasms that I find, as I did in the Botanic Garden project, the best means of communication and the clues to the client's tastes.

Through conversations with other designers, I know that I am not alone in this discovery. Recently, for example, a landscape architect in Milwaukee was discussing with me the difficulty of selling meadow-style plantings to certain clients. His experience in this respect was similar to mine: many clients are strongly drawn to the freedom of such a style, but some are made nervous by the apparent lack of structure. The closely marshaled plants of conventional flower beds offer an obvious pattern; the environmentally adapted tapestry of a meadow garden has an order, too, but it doesn't leap out at the eye. The other designer told me he had found a foolproof way to help clients see what is really there: he shows them reproductions of Georges Seurat's pointillist paintings.

For me, painting, sculpture, music, and the other fine arts are far more than just a sales tool or a means to better understand gardens. The fact is, I find these fields in fundamental ways indistinguishable, as insep-

PATH THROUGH THE IDAHO SCULPTURE
GARDEN DESIGNED BY WILLIAM PETERS.

arably interwoven as the music and dance of a ballet. This complex interrelationship is what most fascinates me about my work. A garden partakes of the other arts and is also uniquely more.

For example, because a garden is in part a scene intended for viewing, its design shares the two-dimensional, depictive quality of painting or drawing. But because it is also a space through which you move, the garden must also be handled as a sculpture. Unlike sculpture, however, a garden is constantly changing, and so, like music and dance, is an art form with a fourth dimension, that of time. In part, this dimension of time and change is a function of how we experience gardens, which is typically as a progression of sights, smells, textures, and views. Managing that involves a process that the gifted San Francisco garden designer William Peters has defined as "choreographing a walk." Through the use of a variety of simple devices, he not only controls where visitors set their feet, but also manipulates the pace at which they move, slowing or speeding their progress, as well as their position, turning the visitors toward or away from the views. I also find it useful to think of gardens in terms of dance. The use of ornamental grasses is one of the signatures of our design style, and I like to dispose these within the landscape in drifts, in part for the rhythmic motion they contribute on a breezy day.

A garden changes through the natural processes of growth and death. The living elements of the garden are always expanding or shrinking, changing color, texture, even form, with the seasons. It's this that makes garden design so uniquely challenging and rewarding. The choreographer or the composer sets the time in a dance or ballad; in the garden, nature keeps the beat, which means that the progress, even for the most expert gardener, is always unpredictable. A garden is always, ultimately, a mystery.

HISTORY

It's worth noting that the interrelationship of gardening with the other arts was taken for granted throughout much of the field's history. When Pope Clement VII wanted a spiritually inspired garden for the villa he was building at the edge of Rome, he naturally turned to the artist who was painting frescoes on the walls of the Vatican, the artist known today as Raphael (and to his contemporaries as Raffaello Sanzio). Why not? The genius for color, composition, and perspective, the understanding of human nature the artist had already demonstrated in his painting were just as important in the design of a garden. Likewise, Clement's contemporary, the French king Francis I, understood that his resident polymath Leonardo da Vinci, with his rare combination of artistic and mechanical virtuosity, was the obvious candidate to design a royal water garden (though, characteristically, Leonardo never finished the project, so that the garden survives only in a sketch).

A couple of centuries later, William Kent used what he had learned from an artistic pilgrimage to Rome to sweep away the fussy, geometrical

THE PRAENESTE, URN, PATHWAY,
AND TREES, ROUSHAM GARDEN,
A SURVIVING MASTERPIECE
BY WILLIAM KENT IN
OXFORDSHIRE, ENGLAND.

formalism of the contemporary English garden. Kent, a former sign painter turned decorator, replaced the unimaginative symmetry he found in clients' gardens with the sort of moody, romantic scenes he had observed in paintings by Salvator Rosa, Gaspard Poussin, and Claude Lorrain. Traditionally trained gardeners were outraged when Kent transplanted (deliberately) a large dead tree to one of his landscapes, but the picturesque effects he dared to create set the stage for a more dramatic, more naturalistic garden style that would sweep through Europe as the *jardin à l'anglais*.

Later yet, toward the end of the nineteenth century, the flowering of the modern English style began when a doctor told the young Gertrude Jekyll that she must spare her failing eyes by giving up the painting and embroidery that she had intended for her life's work. It was her painterly

CLAUDE LORRAIN
(c. 1600–82), *LANDSCAPE WITH MERCHANTS*,
c. 1630. OIL ON CANVAS,
38 1/4" X 56 9/16".
Samuel H. Kress Collection.
Image courtesy of the
National Gallery of Art,
Washington, D.C.

approach to color and texture, the way she used flowers and foliages as pigments to create larger compositions of visual harmony and contrast, that made her subsequent work so admired. In a similar vein, a visit to Giverny reveals not only how much Claude Monet's experience as a painter shaped the garden he made, but also how the understanding of light and color he pursued in the garden influenced his painting.

PERSONAL INSPIRATIONS

Without seeking to put myself on the plane with those masters, I nevertheless believe my own experience also demonstrates the strength that involvement with the other arts can bring to garden design. From early childhood I'd loved planting and growing—my orderly Dutch Calvinist parents watched with dismay, I suspect, as my projects gradually ate up their neatly trimmed lawn. But my formal study of how a landscape organizes itself came on the expeditions I made into the Michigan countryside as a teenager with a neighbor, Margaret Holmes. An elementary school teacher, she'd encouraged me from early childhood to take an interest in the arts, furnishing materials and space to work and allowing me to be messy in a way that would have been unthinkable in my parents' warm but immaculate house. Later, we made a habit of taking paints and easels and driving out to rural spots we found appealing—and in attempting to capture these in two dimensions, I had to analyze and understand what it was about the scenes that made them pleasing. I still believe that this activity provides one of the best ways of learning to really look at a landscape, and I recommend it to all who are interested in sharpening their design skills. Even if your work with brush or pencil displeases you, simply identifying why that is—what is missing in your representation—should help you to better understand the landscape's character.

CLAUDE MONET'S
GARDEN AT GIVERNY,
FRANCE.

Sketching changed from a pastime to a tool when I moved into the study of architecture as a university undergraduate. Sadly, as it became more and more a part of my professional routine, it lost some of its appeal as an avocation. I gained proficiency, but became less inclined to draw just for my own pleasure. This was especially true when, after completing my undergraduate degree at the University of Michigan, I decided to continue as a graduate student in landscape architecture. Now I was sketching landscapes constantly, but always as a means to an end.

Not that my appreciation of a fine line diminished. Indeed, I invested in the pen-and-ink *Portrait of a Child* by Richard Wilt and a lithograph titled *Triton and Psyche* by Emil Weddige, which I still have, while a student at the University of Michigan. I paid what I considered extraordinary sums,

thirty dollars and thirty-five dollars respectively, extravagances I was careful not to reveal to my parents. I wonder, though, if I underestimated them. They were supportive of my decision as a graduate student to transfer to the University of Delft in the Netherlands, and it was there, in that old but vital city, that I learned the importance of indulging your passion.

I spent three years in Delft, a city with a rich cultural heritage that was also, at the beginning of the 1960s, the center of a very dynamic contemporary arts scene. I had the opportunity to meet the painter Jan Schoonhoven, a minimalist member of the Orez Group ("zero" spelled backward), and I became familiar with work of the Cobra Group, which included Karel Appel. I added Schoonhoven's *Cardboard Reliefs* and an Appel gouache to my modest but growing collection. The most important facet of this experience, I believe, was that it taught me that the arts were not

just a luxury for the wealthy, but that they could and should be a part of ordinary people's everyday lives.

I have never lost that conviction, and in 1975 it prompted me to resign from my partnership in a Washington, D.C., urban planning firm and return to my old interest in gardens and garden making. In this I found a kind of completeness I couldn't have anticipated. All my interests and experiences with the arts pulled together in my design, joining with the superb plantsmanship of my new business partner, Wolfgang Oehme, to create the free-form, adventurous style that became known as "the New American Garden." This *is* a genuinely American style, a way of handling the landscape that we drew from the local topography, climate, and soil and the expansive American personality the gardens were intended to fit. But into this I have also mixed the ideas, techniques, and details I have gathered from the Old Master paintings I saw in the Netherlands; the layered sets and gorgeous textiles of Japanese Kabuki theater; ballet and opera; the works of an international cast of contemporary painting and sculpture; even the memories of those Michigan barns and fields I myself tried to capture many years ago. The firm's work continues to evolve as a new generation of talented designers and landscape architects have joined it, each bringing his or her own artistic interests and inspirations to bear on our joint work.

FOR THE GARDENER

I don't consider my cultural interests special. I am intensely drawn to the arts, but then so are most gardeners I have known—in their own way. They may not enjoy Kabuki or bel canto (though I can't imagine life without either); yet nearly all enjoy listening to some sort of music. They read. Quite likely, when on vacation in a foreign city, they spend a day in the art muse-

ums. In the city on business, they pause from time to time in their walk down an avenue to admire the architecture of some particularly striking building. When they shop, they find the fabric and cut of a handsome suit or a glamorous dress exciting, and they surely try on clothes they know they will never buy, just to see, if only briefly, how they might look in another incarnation.

What these other gardeners don't do, typically, is to apply consciously the experiences and techniques they have gathered from other arts to their work on their landscape. They worry about selecting a style, when if they thought about the music that makes their feet want to move (lindy, tango, maybe, or—who knows?—minuet), they'd know just how to direct their steps in the landscape. They don't introduce the textures, hues, and details they have enjoyed at the museum or the boutique. They don't borrow the suspense from the last thriller they read and turn their own landscape into an adventure (one with a happy ending, of course).

Instead of taking advantage of all these accumulated tools, we routinely fall back on horticultural rules of thumb and clichés. The rationale seems to be that if we do what everyone else does, we won't do any worse. Or maybe we pick up one of those books on "plant partners," those compilations of tables and lists that recommend plants that may be combined without giving visual offense. They remind me of the menus you used to find in the Chinese restaurants of my youth, which selected your meal for you: "one from column A, two from column B."

Such a mechanical approach to garden design ensures a passionless, mediocre result. And, it's no fun.

It's not difficult to change this situation. You don't have to pursue a long course of study or take out a subscription to the Philharmonic (though you might find a seat in the dress circle a pleasant break from digging and planting). For the most part, all you need to do is to reapply the interests and skills that you already possess.

That is easy enough to do. I can help you make this transition by sharing some of the experiences I have had in the course of my thirty-year career in garden design. I'll add to this the insights of my partners. You'll find all these experiences detailed in the following pages, presented as case studies in which I discuss ways I drew on specific artworks or the techniques of a particular artist or art form to organize, plant, and decorate a garden. I've alternated the case studies with short essays, more general looks at art forms I have found pertinent with descriptions of how I have found that genre's principles to apply to garden design.

Finally, I've also followed a practice that is the standby of all successful garden designers: where special knowledge was needed, I've consulted experts. To present a broader range of insights, I spoke with a range of artists whose work I admire, from the cellist Yo-Yo Ma to the sculptor Grace Knowlton, from the internationally recognized textile designer Jack Lenor Larsen to the painter Robert Dash, all virtuosos whom I also know to be involved in one way or another with gardening. I've asked these extraordinary individuals how the skills they developed in one field have translated to the landscape art, and what advice they could give to the rest of us gardeners.

Join with me, then. Grab your sketch pad, your brushes, and your palette. Lace up your dancing shoes, tune your instrument, and sharpen your spade. Let's garden with the arts.

THE ARTFUL GARDEN

A HOME ON THE EASTERN
SHORE OF MARYLAND
DESIGNED BY SUMAN SORG.

SPACE AND FORM

We don't even learn form through the eyes;
we learn it through the sense of touch.

—John Sloan (1871–1951),
American painter of
the Ashcan School

We turn clay to make a vessel;
But it is on the space where there is nothing
that the usefulness of the vessel depends.

—Lao Tzu

GAZEBO BY BEN FORGEY
ON MARYLAND'S
EASTERN SHORE.

When I begin the process of designing a garden for a new or returning client it often occurs to me that there is a fundamental problem with the tools we use for this process. In the standard fashion of landscape architects and garden designers, I reach for a pencil and spread a fresh sheet of paper on my drawing table. These tools, however, can represent a garden only in two dimensions, as a pattern of lines, shapes, and sym-

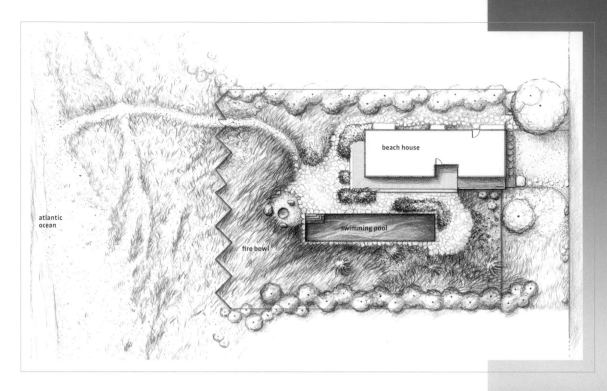

OCEANSIDE GARDEN ON
THE SOUTH SHORE OF
LONG ISLAND, NEW YORK.

bols or as a series of views. I am working in two dimensions. Yet a garden is by its nature a creation in three dimensions (or even four; for more about this, see chapter 6).

I'm not suggesting that we abandon the use of garden plans. To attack any complex landscape project without first mapping it out graphically would be as foolish as trying to build a house without a blueprint. And yet, I think that a garden maker should include an extra step at the very beginning of the creative process. Rather than starting with a two-dimensional representation, the designer should spend some time first thinking of the garden in its full three dimensions. Spend time exploring the landscape, im-

VIEW TOWARD THE
ATLANTIC OCEAN
WITH SWIMMING
POOL IN FORE-
GROUND AND BEACH
HOUSE ON THE RIGHT.

ABOVE: **FIRE PIT IN FOREGROUND, BEACH HOUSE ON THE LEFT.**

OPPOSITE: **VIEW FROM THE BEACH HOUSE OVER THE SWIMMING POOL TOWARD THE OCEAN.**

merse yourself in it so that you become intimately familiar with its shape and character. Imagine what you will create as a grand, living piece of sculpture. It's the interaction between the land and the experience you hope to construct there that should dictate the garden's lines and forms. Like a sculptor, you need to imagine this in three dimensions.

I find this approach to be helpful in a couple of ways. In the first place, it allows me to focus on the first goal of garden design, which is to create a strong and appropriate structure of integrated spaces and forms. Gardeners tend to think of gardens as collections of plants. That's understandable; I, too, was first attracted to this field by the sensual enjoyment plants offer, the colors and perfumes of flowers, the lush shades of foliages, the textures of barks. But unless we discipline these experiences with an organized, carefully conceived structure, the pleasures subside into chaos. The garden becomes a random stew in which the flavors com-

pete rather than cooperate. This is why, in the initial stages of the planning process, you need to set aside your dreams of planting and adopt, at least temporarily, the sculptor's more abstract focus on forms and shapes and how they will relate to each other. Think of the garden as a composition of masses (objects) and voids (empty spaces). Simplifying your vision in this way allows you to concentrate on disciplining the space, on laying down the structure around which the garden can grow.

Another reason for thinking of the garden as sculpture is that it encourages restraint. Like most gardeners, I'm very susceptible to the beauties of plants, easily seduced by any new species I encounter. But I long ago learned that it is a mistake to treat space, as so many gardeners do, as if it is elastic. It's been my experience that gardeners are prone to believe that there is always room for another specimen, that no matter how full the garden is, with a bit of ingenuity we can find space for just one more. This does both the garden and the plants an injustice. Plants need room to grow and develop, and their truest beauty emerges only when they are properly related one to another and to the landscape in which they are set. I don't know if Michelangelo Buonarroti liked babies, but suppose he did: imagine the effect it would have had on the *Pietà* if he had decided to insert a couple more cute infants into the Madonna's lap. Or if Auguste Rodin, unable to choose among models, had created a milling mob of pensive figures instead of a single powerful nude, chin on fist, as *The Thinker*.

These are all reasons why I return again and again to the works of my favorite sculptors as aids to my own garden design. If you've never interested yourself in this art form, now—before you start digging and planting—would be a good time to do so. Visit the nearest museum or private gallery and look at what they offer in the way of three-dimensional works. Try to suspend your feelings about categories such as figurative versus abstract, traditional versus avant-garde, and let yourself react to the individ-

ual works in a purely emotional way. Find the ones with which you feel comfortable. Then analyze what it is that appeals to you about those pieces.

What you'll find, I believe, is that you are reacting to how the artist has balanced or set in opposition the different masses, and also the spaces that he or she has chosen to leave empty. It is the handling of these elements that gives character to the piece as a whole, that transmits an experience from the artist to the viewer.

I should at this point include a warning. A garden also differs in a fundamental respect from most sculpture. Sculpture, with some important exceptions, consists of space that the artist has shaped from the outside—the sculptor stands outside the block of marble as he chisels, outside the complex of steel as she welds another element—and it is intended to be experienced that way. The viewer is on the outside looking in. A garden, however, is a habitat, a complex that is constructed from the inside and that is meant to be experienced from the inside. This distinction makes the act of conceiving a garden somewhat different: you must visualize its space from the interior, imagining it as if you are already moving through it.

Even in this respect, though, you can learn much from sculptural artists. One of the most famous artists of the twentieth century was the English sculptor Henry Moore. His enigmatic monumental bronzes adorn so many plazas and parks around the United States that almost anyone who keeps their eyes open while they travel will have seen at least one example of Moore's work. It's appropriate that his pieces should be so often displayed outdoors, for like a good garden designer, Moore understood the importance of taking the onlooker through his spaces and around his masses. Early in his career, he discovered the power that he could give to his sculptures by piercing them with holes that opened up the bulk, taking the onlooker inside the experience and so turning what could have been a passive experience into a journey. It was this, in part, that attracted Moore to working in bronze. Because this material is cast rather than carved, Moore could manipulate the shapes more easily, exploring the effect of passages of different sizes, contours, and directions.

Moore derived many of his forms from female figures, and the sculptor took to sectioning these, arranging the pieces with calculated gaps. As he once explained, "The two- and three-piece sculptures were experiments and you must experiment. You do things in which you eliminate something which is perhaps essential, but to learn how essential it is you leave it out. The space then becomes very significant. . . . If you are doing a reclining figure you just do the head and the legs. You leave space for the body, imagining the other part even though it isn't there. The space then becomes very expressive and you have to get it just right."

POSITIVE VERSUS NEGATIVE SPACE

> A garden isn't complete until nothing
> more can be removed.
>
> —Japanese proverb

As I noted at the beginning of the chapter, we commonly work in two dimensions when we design a garden. Because of this, we tend to think of gardens in terms of linear patterns, most often as symmetrical and asymmetrical arrangements of objects—"formal" or "informal," in gardeners' parlance. There is value in this practice. The lines created by paths or flower borders, walls or hedges, are powerful devices. They form axes that pull the eye down and through a landscape and can be used to direct the eye toward some calculated view. The creation of patterns and their repetition across the landscape creates rhythms, and in the landscape as in music, rhythm is a potent tool for creating mood and drama.

Still, when you are just beginning to design your garden, there is another kind of distinction and contrast that, at this stage of the process, is more important. That is the distinction between positive and negative space.

These are sculptor's terms. "Positive space" is the area of a composi-

tion occupied by an object or mass—in a garden, the positive space would be rocks, trees, shrubs, or any other plant, even landforms such as a knoll or hill. "Negative space" is any area of the composition (or garden) which isn't occupied by an object.

Gardeners tend to focus exclusively on the elements of positive space: that is, the objects and plants they can put into the garden. A skilled sculptor, however, understands the importance and power of the negative space. It is with this that the sculptor defines form. Michelangelo recognized this when he described his sculptural practice as one of gradually revealing with his chisel the form that was contained in the stone block—he viewed the process as methodically increasing the negative space. Giorgio Vasari, a painter who knew Michelangelo personally and who is remembered today less for his own art than for *Lives of the Artists*, the book he wrote about his more talented contemporaries, defined sculpture as "an art which by removing all that is superfluous from the material under treatment reduces it to that form designed in the artist's mind."

A contemporary sculptor who thoroughly understands the power of negative space, and actively creates it, is Joel Shapiro. He works in strong industrial materials such as I-beams, fashioning lines and frames that command the space. In realizing his visions, he strips away everything that isn't essential, so that our view is reduced to the pure form, the space itself that the sculpture is defining. I've included a number of his pieces in gardens I've designed for clients, and I particularly enjoy the contrast between Shapiro's treatment of space and the work of another sculptor I admire: Fernando Botero.

The work of this Colombian artist is massive and self-contained, like a rock that invites closer inspection and interpretation. His sculptures unquestionably create positive space and an image upon which the viewer is free to project his own moods and opinions. These wonderful

lumps often make me smile, and their sensuous curves delight the eye. As solid as they are, Botero's works can also be critically placed in a garden setting to serve a directional function, to point the way or call attention to a special area.

Negative space is more than just an absence of material, however. It's also the frame you use to set off forms within the sculpture or garden. The work of Martin Puryear, the brilliant contemporary sculptor from Washington, D.C., wonderfully illustrates this concept. As a young man, Puryear studied crafts and worked in wood, creating various utilitarian objects such as guitars, furniture, and canoes. The techniques he learned in this way he carried over into his sculpture—he works in many media, but has returned again and again to simple materials such as strips of wood or wire, with which he can indicate a shape or form with the very minimum of structure. Puryear's art appeals to me because it is so concise: a piece is often more striking for what isn't there than for what is.

Negative space can be just as powerful in the garden. It is the negative space of the sky, for example, that lends power to the silhouette of a tree. Negative space also serves to balance the weight of the objects in the garden, the positive spaces. It tempers the impact of the forms and masses, and in doing so it contributes to setting the mood of sculpture and garden alike. An abundance of negative space creates a spare, often stately feeling. The regal impact of Louis XIV's palace landscape at Versailles, for example, derives not so much from its trees as from the broad, open allées that they frame. Keeping the negative space to a minimum can make a garden feel cozy, but if carried to excess it will make the landscape feel crowded and busy, as claustrophobic as a knickknack-and-doily-filled Victorian parlor.

MARTIN PURYEAR,
BRUNHILDE. INSTALLATION
VIEW FROM THE MARTIN
PURYEAR EXHIBITION,
EAST BUILDING ATRIUM,
NATIONAL GALLERY OF ART,
2008. National Gallery of Art,
Washington, D.C.,
Gallery Archives.

THE MASTERS OF
NEGATIVE GARDEN SPACE

In my experience, the greatest masters in the use of negative space in garden design are the Japanese. I suspect this derives from the influence on their work of Zen Buddhism. Zen was imported from China to Japan in the twelfth and thirteenth centuries A.D. and brought with it a belief that self-knowledge could (and should) be pursued not only through meditation but also through self-expression in the fine arts—which among the Japanese included garden design. Indeed, skill at garden design was considered by the adepts of this sect to be a fine art on a par with painting, and artists often moved back and forth between these two disciplines. Painters sought inspiration for their landscape paintings in famous gardens, and garden designers applied what they had learned as painters to the composition of landscapes. One could argue that rearranging the land-scape was really the primary sculptural tradition of Zen.

The linking of gardening to spiritual self-knowledge gave the Zen gar-dens a unique style. The object of Zen practice is to return to a conscious-ness of the essential nature of things, a goal that is accomplished by the deliberate peeling away of superficialities. To achieve the experience of spiritual awakening that followers of Zen seek, it is necessary to practice (they believe) a letting go of self. You must empty yourself of ego and at-tachments. Given that philosophy, it should not be surprising that Zen gardens are as remarkable for what they don't include as for what they do. One of the most famous examples, the garden at the Ryoan-ji temple in Kyoto, contains only fifteen stones in a sea of gravel.

RYOAN-JI GARDEN,
KYOTO, JAPAN.

Set in a courtyard adjoining the temple's main hall, this is a highly abstract composition. Classed by Japanese experts as belonging to the "dry landscape" or *karesansui* style, the Ryoan-ji garden is one of restrained allusions: water, for instance, is suggested by stylized ripples raked into the courtyard's bed of gravel. Whereas mosses might well be overlooked in a lusher landscape, here, because they are the only planting, they have a powerful impact. Likewise, because the landscape has been reduced to the absolute minimum of elements, the negative spaces—the silences between the notes—speak up most eloquently here. Like the silence of the Zendo, the hall dedicated to meditation, the negative spaces of the garden seem to quiet the mind and draw viewers out of themselves almost hypnotically.

Interestingly, a study published in the British scientific journal *Nature* in 2002 suggests another means by which the garden's negative spaces affect the mood of the visitor. The placement of the stones, the positive spaces, is asymmetrical and not apparently coordinated with the geometry of the surrounding buildings. Using a computer analysis of the negative spaces, however, a trio of researchers at Kyoto University found that the axes—the lines created by the relationships of the voids—form an image like the skeleton of a tree, with the trunk running through the primary vantage point from which the garden was designed to be viewed.

I very much doubt that this pattern was a conscious creation of the garden's designer, the unknown genius who supervised the installation of this garden half a millennium ago. Still, it seems unlikely to have been accidental, since to move even one cluster of rocks within the space would destroy this extraordinary relationship of the negative spaces. Perhaps the monastic gardener found his way to this design unconsciously, through the sort of meditative process that is the heart of Zen practice. It's worth noting that scientists have found that even when onlookers do not consciously perceive such hidden patterns, they still react to them, and it seems probable that part of the mysterious emotional power that the Ryoan-ji garden famously has on visitors is a result of the design of its negative spaces.

Few of us would adopt such a spare, austere style in our own garden. Personally, I'm more comfortable in the lush, meadowlike setting of my firm's "New American Garden" style. Still, when I design, I keep in mind the lessons I have learned during trips to Japan.

DEREK JARMAN'S GARDEN

The Japanese designers aren't the only masters of the use of negative space, of course. A notable contemporary example can be found in the garden that British artist and filmmaker Derek Jarman created on England's southeast coast, at Dungeness. The site, an open expanse of pebbles on

DEREK JARMAN'S GARDEN. A VIEW TOWARD PROSPECT HOUSE ON DUNGENESS BEACH.

the beach, within view of the silos of a nuclear power station, is powerful but bleak; appropriately so, for Jarman began the garden soon after he was diagnosed with an incurable, fatal disease. Instead of enclosing the space, Jarman chose to emphasize its exposure, punctuating the unfenced space with low sculptures he created out of stones, driftwood, and flotsam he found along the shore, and with native or naturalized plants such as sea kale, lavender, and dog roses that could withstand the wind and spray. This odd collection, retrieved from the water's edge by a man who faced an ebbing of his own tide, is given an uncanny power by the way it floats like an island amid a seemingly endless stretch of sky, sea, and emptiness.

NEGATIVE AND POSITIVE SPACE IN THE NEW AMERICAN GARDEN

Not all uses of negative space need be so dramatic, nor do they necessarily emphasize the emptiness of a landscape. In the work of our firm, we more often aim for a balance, using the voids to emphasize and reinforce the effect of the masses and vice versa.

An example of this was the design we arrived at for the setting of the National World War II Memorial that was built on the Mall in Washington, D.C. When we joined the project, it was meeting with intense criticism from many members of the public because its architectural elements—a circular array of stone pillars, walls, and a pavilion—would visually interrupt the broad, open sweep of lawn stretching from the Lincoln Memorial to the Washington Monument. In other words, it would violate the site's grand and inspiring negative space. Architect Friedrich St. Florian's response to this concern was a stroke of genius (in fact, it was what won him the commission). He proposed dropping the floor of the monument six feet below the surface of the surrounding ground. This minimized the Memorial's im-

THE FOUNTAIN AT THE
WORLD WAR II MEMORIAL
ON THE NATIONAL MALL IN
WASHINGTON, D.C.,
LOOKING WEST TOWARD
THE LINCOLN MEMORIAL.
© Robert Lautman, courtesy of
the National Building Museum.

pact on its surroundings without compromising the monumental proportions of the architecture that the dignity of the memorial demanded.

Another project that demonstrates how to use mass and void to reinforce each other is the landscape we designed as a setting for a client's country retreat on the Eastern Shore of the Chesapeake Bay in Maryland. The 85-acre property abuts the shore of the Tred Avon River, and its greatest asset was the expansive views across the water. When we began work, however, the site was otherwise uninspiring. There were some fine old trees, but the house, a handsome classical Georgian revival, seemed marooned amid a flat, relatively featureless expanse of lawn. Essentially, the

landscape was a nearly uniform expanse of negative space, and not at all inviting for that reason.

There was an obvious need to restore the balance of mass and void. As Eric Groft, the principal from our firm who took charge of this project, decided in consultation with the owners, our role would be to define different areas within this space, enclosing them to create a series of more intimate experiences. At the same time, because the clients love to entertain on a generous scale, they wanted to preserve the open space between the house and water, not just to maintain the views from the house but also to make sure there was room to erect a tent for outdoor parties. A further complication was a local code that forbids new construction within a 100-foot setback from the water's edge (though it did permit the creation of a series of formal verandas along the river side of the house, spaces that were designed as outdoor extensions of interior rooms and galleries).

The obvious way to structure such a relatively featureless site is to create enclosures with walls or fences, or their green equivalent, hedges. By blocking views, however, such structures would detract from the property's chief visual attraction and rupture the connection between land and water. We chose instead to use massed perennials and grasses, statuesque, head-high species such as *Molinia, Erianthus, Panicum virgatum,* and *Hibiscus moscheuto,* to informally enclose the different areas—the swimming pool and pool terrace, a forecourt, a dining terrace off the kitchen, a secret garden off the master bedroom, a veranda with an open-air spa, a formal cutting and vegetable garden, and the guesthouse. We also used these plantings to frame the central lawn that stretched from house to shore. Together, the perennials and grasses created the essential sense of mass and yet remained visually permeable, allowing glimpses of the areas beyond, inviting exploration. Indeed, the lady of the house calls her new landscape "the garden of the seven veils" because of its seductive sense of mystery and invitation.

Like the holes with which Henry Moore pierced his sculptures, inter-penetrations of void and mass can enhance the power and interest of a landscape. In this garden on the Eastern Shore, we redesigned the swimming pool to give it a more natural elliptical form and preserved the view from the pool to the river. We dropped the edge on the river side of the pool so that the water seems to spill out over it, making the pool appear to be an extension of the natural water body beyond.

Our most explicit play on space was an outdoor sitting room that we placed next to one of the guesthouses on the estate. This was inspired by an existing concrete pad between the house and river, which had survived whatever was originally built on it and served no purpose. We knew, however, that the codes regulating waterside construction dictated that if the pad were removed, nothing else could be installed in its place. So we commissioned sculptor Ben Forgey to create on it a modernist folly, a cage of bleached timbers. This defined the seating area within, creating a sense of protection, but it also left the area open to the surrounding space so that those relaxing there could feel connected to the water, birds, and sky.

OPPORTUNITIES OF FORM AND SCALE

A successful plant combination relies
primarily on shapes.

—PIET OUDOLF, CONTEMPORARY
DUTCH ARCHITECT TURNED
NURSERYMAN, CREATOR OF
THE "NEW WAVE" STYLE OF
GARDEN DESIGN

How you balance mass and void helps to determining the emotional impact of a landscape. But there is another aspect to this interaction that

the garden maker should also keep in mind. Their intersection—the meeting of mass and void—is what creates the surfaces that we see as form. In gardener's jargon, form is typically used to connote the profile of a plant: a spruce has a "conical" or "pyramidal" form according to the nursery catalog, while that of a prostrate juniper is "creeping." When designing the garden as a whole, however, it helps to extend this sort of analysis to all the objects in the garden, from rocks to trees to architectural elements, because the relationship between these forms—harmonious, contrasting, or even discordant—sets the basic character of the landscape.

As any accomplished sculptor knows, different types of forms inspire different emotional reactions, so manipulation of form becomes a powerful tool (perhaps the most powerful) for shaping a visitor's experience of the garden. Subtle, sinuous curves are what give a classical Greek Aphrodite her erotic sensuality—an utterly different impact than that of a Giacometti's tense, tautly stretched musculature. The effects of different forms is a distinction gardeners need to understand and a device they can use in their own gardens. The best way to learn it is to spend some time in the sculpture gallery of the nearest art museum, paying attention to how your feelings change as you move from piece to piece.

Scale is an easier concept to grasp. When applied to artworks and gardens, it refers to the relative proportion of different elements of a composition to each other and to their setting. Looking at the work of an unskilled artist, actually, is the quickest way to learn the importance of scale. Why is that portrait so disturbing? The head is just a bit too large for the torso. It's out of scale. Or the eyes are too large for the face, or too small. Similarly, in a garden, siting a burly evergreen tree in a small court violates the scale of the setting. The planting overwhelms, it makes the visitor feel not refreshed but nervous. A broad flight of steps ends in a narrow path—

the scale of the two elements does not agree. The steps look pumped up on steroids and the path unpleasantly meager.

Of course, a deliberate, calculated violation of scale can be effective, too. The ancient Egyptian pharaoh Rameses II commissioned four monumental sculptural portraits of himself, each 20 meters high, to grace the façade of the temple he built at Abu Simbel. Though portrayed as seated, the pharaoh's doppelgangers still tower over the portraits of wife, mother, and children clustered around their knees. The message about who dominates is plain. In a similar, though less megalomaniacal, vein, I've often played tricks with scale, using a large plant to emphasize the compact nature of a space, or using delicate ones to make the setting feel more expansive or rugged.

BARBARA HEPWORTH
(1903–75), BRONZE
SCULPTURE IN
A GARDEN SETTING.

A SCULPTOR'S GARDEN
A VISIT WITH GRACE KNOWLTON

I cannot think of a greater compliment a garden maker can pay to a sculptor: I've included works by Grace Knowlton in both of my personal gardens. I included three of her irregular, hand-built spheres in the garden I created in the tiny backyard of my former townhouse in Washington's Georgetown district. They provided visual focal points and more—at night, with the garden softly illuminated by floodlights, it seemed as if a flock of moons had come to roost there.

More recently, I included two of Grace's spheres in the garden at Ferry Cove, the weekend retreat I built on the eastern shore of the Chesapeake Bay. One sphere is of rough-textured concrete; that one is poised on a wide spot in the oyster-shell path to the house's front door. The other I have placed indoors—it helps to link the interior of the house to the garden and blur what I see as an unnecessary distinction between the two. Pieced together from copper, the interior sphere has a patina that exactly matches the hue of the pickled wood floor; set between the living and dining spaces, it punctuates and visually divides what is actually one large room.

I met Grace at a benefit at the Corcoran Gallery in Washington in 1982. A year later, relatively early in the history of my partnership with

Wolfgang Oehme, she called us. She wanted us to create a garden around her house—a barn on New York's Hudson River Palisades that had been renovated by the architect Hugh Hardy.

Grace has worked in many media, in particular as a painter, photographer, and ceramicist. But by the time I met her, she was focused on three-dimensional work and had embarked on what has proved to be her most persistent theme. She had begun to fashion spheres—rough and smooth, large and small, from different materials, juxtaposing them against each other and against their surroundings.

Her use of this form is supremely simple and yet endlessly suggestive. In different settings and iterations, Grace's spheres call to mind the earth and sun, or a seed, or, as I have said, the moon. Recently, when I mentioned this mutability to Grace, she spoke of the "primal connection" she believes most people feel toward this form. It is, she added, a simple, if not the most simple, shape, and as such it invites people to project onto it their own moods. This gives her spherical sculptures a chameleon quality. They change character with the daily progress of sunlight and shadow, with every snowfall and thaw.

When I asked Grace how her fascination with this form arose, she replied that it was "certainly completely unconscious," but that "in retrospect [it was due to the fact that] I was pregnant." She had been moving from painting on flat surfaces to three-dimensional ones, and had begun using clay to fashion the shapes on which she could apply her colors.

"I began to have this overpowering urge to close the form. I thought, What was this about? What it was, was the idea of capturing the space. That just blew my mind, that you could close space in. . . . Magic.

"Then later," she added, " I began to think of them, that I was inside them" (understandable, given her physical condition at the time), "and that [like the developing child] I was protected by this armor."

Grace quickly abandoned the idea of using her hand-shaped spheres as canvases for colors and glazes. That, she recalled, looked "forced, crafty." She preferred to let the materials—ceramic, metallic, or concrete—speak for themselves. She moved out of the cocoon, shattering spheres or cutting holes in them. That, she confessed, felt "dangerous." But, she continued, "I was getting brave and related to the outside."

Literally. She found that her spheres became "powerful presences" outdoors in the landscape. They played especially well with the sweeps of perennials and grasses Wolfgang and I were planting for her; the compact geometrical shapes were the perfect foil for the soft textures of the planting and the simple verticals of the grasses. Grace noticed that the spheres seemed to set the mood of the garden and that they struck different viewers very differently; she suspected that the simple, featureless shapes were functioning as screens onto which visitors projected their feelings. And unlike the stones, which serve as metaphors for permanence and once placed are usually left as set, Grace enjoyed moving the spheres, grouping and regrouping them to change the geometry of the scene. Incidentally, not all the moves were calculated: a graduate student who had rented a cottage on the property later told me how he was startled as he walked home late one windy night by a large and lightweight metal-clad sphere rolling across his path, driven by the gusts.

Personally, I find these forms to be the very definition of focus, and as such they have a galvanizing effect on a landscape. By giving a scene a visual center, they pull it together spatially. This is why I've so often shared Grace's sculpture with clients. I placed a selection as a temporary exhibit in a high-end shopping complex on Long Island whose landscape I designed. They fit perfectly into this highly architectural setting. Yet another, a sphere four feet in diameter, worked equally well as a serene counterpoint to the twisting trunks of olive trees and whorled green agave rosettes in the garden my firm contributed to CornerStone Sonoma, a famous West Coast gallery of outdoor installations by garden and landscape designers.

"The idea of [sculpture and plants] working together," says Grace, "that's what I love. The interplay that adds life."

2

LIGHT AND SHADOW

Look at light and admire its beauty. Close your eyes, and then look again: what you saw is no longer there; and what you will see later is not yet.

—Leonardo da Vinci

For me, a landscape does not exist in its own right, since its appearance changes at every moment; but the surrounding atmosphere brings it to life—the light and the air which vary continually. For me, it is only the surrounding atmosphere which gives subjects their true value.

—Claude Monet

A COPPER BOWL SEEMS TO DROP WATER FROM THE LILY POOL TO THE SWIMMING POOL; HOWEVER, THE WATER IS RECIRCULATING FROM THE SWIMMING POOL SO IT'S A "FOOL-YOUR-EYE EFFECT."

Quick: select a pivotal area of your garden, one of the most visible or most used locations, and tell me (without stepping outside to check) what the light is like there in the morning, at noon, and in midafternoon. What is the light like there in the spring, summer, fall, winter?

This is a trick question, really—almost no gardener carries this sort of information around in his or her head. Yet understanding light, not just in general but also in the particular, is crucial to successful garden design. Vision, after all, is the primary sense through which we experience the world around us, and light is the medium of vision. Change the light, and the appearance of a scene can change drastically. The delicate pastel colors that are so pleasantly harmonious in the softer, clear light of morning are likely to seem washed out and weak in the stronger, harsher light of midday or of high summer. Stronger hues—bright reds and yellows, for example—show up better in that light. Yet as the day comes to an end and the light fades at dusk, the brighter colors seem to darken. Our eyes sense blue-green light more readily at low levels, and at dusk you'll typically notice the landscape taking on a bluish hue, and blue flowers will seem to glow.

GARDENS DESIGNED TO BE VIEWED IN SPECIFIC LIGHTS

My firm prides itself on the versatility of the gardens we create. As a rule, we design landscapes that are inviting and rewarding at every time of day and for every season, that can complement almost every mood and accommodate a wide range of activities. Still, I have been intrigued by a number of gardens I have come across over the years that were intentionally designed to suit one particular time of day: morning, evening, even nighttime. Typically, these gardens achieve their specialized effects by adapting to the particular kind of light that distinguishes the time of day for which they are designed.

The night gardens, for instance (what I like to think of as horticultural nocturnes), are classically planted with white flowers that show well

THE SWIMMING POOL, LILY POOL, AND FOUNTAIN ARE CENTERED ON THE DINING ROOM WINDOW IN THIS GEORGETOWN GARDEN IN WASHINGTON, D.C.

in the silvery, weaker light of the moon. The concept of a white garden, a space filled with white flowers and silver foliages, was pioneered in the first half of the last century by the great English gardeners Lawrence Johnston (of Hidcote Manor in Gloucestershire) and Vita Sackville-West, the doyenne of Sissinghurst Castle in Kent. Neither of these two famous gardens, so far as I know, was conceived with the explicit idea of nocturnal visits, though in a newspaper column Sackville-West wrote about her plans for this space, "All the same, I cannot help hoping that the great ghostly barn-owl will sweep silently across a pale garden, next summer, in the twilight—the pale garden that I am now planting, under the first flakes of snow." In any event, the fact that this type of garden, though pallid by daylight, takes on a special chaste air of mystery and elegance by moonlight has resulted in their being billed as "moon gardens" or "night gardens" in their succeeding incarnations.

When visiting such gardens, I cannot help thinking that their color schemes, or at least the awareness of what darkness does to our perception of a landscape, may owe much, at least indirectly, to the pioneering work of the nineteenth-century American expatriate painter James McNeill Whistler and the paintings he also called his "nocturnes," such as *Nocturne: Blue and Gold—Old Battersea Bridge* and *Nocturne in Black and Gold: The Falling Rocket*. These scenes, mostly of London, outraged late Victorian critics with the way they dissolved form into patterns of light and dark. With their bluish tones punctuated by bursts of white and the erasure of almost all other colors, however, they offer an invaluable tutorial for any gardener seeking to design a garden space that will be attractive after sunset as well as before.

Whistler's famous contemporary, the French Impressionist painter Claude Monet, pursued the analysis of light to an almost obsessive degree. He calculated that the light changed every seven minutes in his garden at

Giverny, the subject of many of his paintings during the last decades of his life. He would set up several canvases, sometimes as many as ten or even twenty, at one spot, recording his impression of that view on one for a few minutes, then switching to the next as he noticed the light changing with the progress of the day, and then on to the next and the next. He'd work in this fashion day after day to ensure that when all the paintings were finished, each would be absolutely authentic to one kind of light.

What is most interesting for a gardener about Monet's preoccupation with the quality of different lights is that he translated it from the canvas to the landscape. He planted a "sunset border" at Giverny, a rectangular tangle of yellow, gold, orange, and mahogany wallflowers (*Cheiranthus*) and red columbines (*Aquilegia*) toward the west side of the garden, knowing that these colors would explode when backlit by the red light of sunset. He balanced this with a "sunrise border" on the garden's east side, a bed of pastels—pink and blue columbines, for example, pink lupines and mauve tulips, that astonish with their delicate contrasts in the crisp light of early morning.

GEOGRAPHY AND LIGHT

Regional differences in light are one reason why it rarely works to re-create in your own landscape a garden style you've admired while vacationing in different parts of this country or the world. One of the most interesting failures of this kind I've seen was the exhibit that designer Yves St. Laurent created for the 1997 Chelsea Flower Show. If you've never been to that horticultural extravaganza held every May in London, you should— it's a sort of World Series of gardening, a venue at which the leading gardeners of Europe and even the United States vie to outdo each other in displays of horticultural rarities and design virtuosity. St. Laurent re-

HENRI MATISSE (1869–1954), *OPEN WINDOW, COLLIOURE*, 1905. OIL ON CANVAS, 21 3/4" X 18 1/8". Collection of Mr. and Mrs. John Hay Whitney. Image courtesy of the National Gallery of Art, Washington, D.C. © 2010 Succession H. Matisse / Artists Rights Society (ARS), New York.

created in his exhibit a scene from the Majorelle Garden in the Moroccan city of Marrakech. Majorelle was a locally famous garden created in the early years of the twentieth century by an expatriate French painter; St. Laurent had rescued this gem after the founder's death and turned it into a botanical garden with a museum housing a collection of Islamic art. Majorelle is, by all accounts (I've never been there), a bit of paradise, a collage of brilliant colors that gleam in the desert sun. But when St. Laurent transferred these colors without adjustment to cool, cloudy London, they seemed merely lurid. The whole exhibit reminded me of a teenage girl's overly enthusiastic experiment with makeup.

In fairness to St. Laurent, his mistake (if you can call it that—his exhibit did make Majorelle a major travel destination) is one that has been repeated endlessly by gardeners everywhere. Visit any of the English-style gardens of Southern California. To surround your home with the trappings of an old-world manor house was a popular demonstration of personal success in the heyday of 1920s Hollywood glamour. Visit one of the survivors— Marston House Garden in San Diego's Balboa Park is a fine example—and you'll find that in the harsher California sunlight, the green of the turf and the colors of the flowers are too fully exposed, too well lit. What was subtle and romantic in Gertrude Jekyll's England acquired a Disney-like obviousness and artificiality in Hollywood.

By now perhaps you are feeling that this is all too complicated. But, fortunately, the problems of understanding the local light and figuring out how to use it to best advantage have already been worked out, and the solutions posted for your examination.

Visit a regional art museum and study the work of landscape painters who have worked in your region. Georgia O'Keeffe spent almost sixty years exploring how light interacted with form and color in New Mexico. Why not learn from her paintings how important form becomes in

GEORGIA O'KEEFFE
(1887–1986), *UNTITLED
(RED AND YELLOW CLIFFS)*,
1940. OIL ON CANVAS, 24" X 36".
Georgia O'Keeffe Museum,
gift of The Burnett Foundation.
© 2010 Georgia O'Keeffe
Museum / Artists Rights Society
(ARS), New York

the crystal-clear, unforgiving desert light? How strong and assertive the colors are, how stark the contrasts? A Northeastern gardener could do far worse than spend some time with the paintings of the Hudson River School. Whether or not you enjoy the romantic, spiritual vision of those painters—Thomas Cole, Frederic Church, and their lesser-known colleagues—they understood very well how that region's hazy atmosphere and misty skies softened hard edges and provided a perfect background for subtle harmonies and contrasts of cooler greens and blues.

An artist whose understanding of light especially inspires me is Henri Matisse, a leading figure in the early-twentieth-century group that critics dubbed *les fauves*, "the wild beasts," for the violent colors of their paintings ("sticks of dynamite" was how one admirer described the hues). Matisse, who was born and raised in the cloudy north of France, kept moving south in search of more brilliant light and the incandescent colors it evoked. He found the intensity he sought on the French Riviera, painting many of the local landscapes. The subject of a painting was unimportant for him, he claimed. "Light . . . expressed by a harmony of intensely colored surfaces" was his goal. As such, his paintings wonderfully capture the atmosphere of that sun-drenched region. It is said that Matisse would wear sunglasses as he painted these landscapes because he was afraid he would go blind from staring so long at the southern colors. If I were gardening in our own Southwest, it is from Matisse's canvases I would take my palette.

Don't limit your studies only to masters. The representations of your region by lesser-known artists, the works you'll find at local art shows, can be just as informative. Analyze what rings true in their paintings or drawings and what doesn't. Recognizing which of their color schemes or treatments of forms seem inauthentic to the local landscape can save you from making the same mistakes.

ATMOSPHERIC PERSPECTIVE

Another useful lesson to be learned from painters about the use of light seems to have originated with the great master of the Italian Renaissance, Leonardo da Vinci. It was what he called "the perspective of disappearance." In one of his famous coded notebooks, Leonardo wrote:

> An object will appear more or less distinct at the same distance, in proportion as the atmosphere existing between the eye and that object is more or less clear. Hence, as I know that the greater or less quantity of the air that lies between the eye and the object makes the outlines of that object more or less indistinct, you must diminish the definiteness of outline of those objects in proportion to their increasing distance from the eye of the spectator.

What Leonardo had discovered is a phenomenon that today is called *aerial perspective*. What this entails, essentially, is that as light travels through the atmosphere, it is diffracted and weakened by particles of dust or moisture suspended in the air. For this reason, the light reflected off distant objects is weaker when it reaches our eyes than the light reflected off nearby ones. The result is that the color of the distant objects becomes less intense, and the forms less distinct. Most often, the change in the color is a bluing or graying of distant objects, though at sunset or dawn, when the sun fills the light with orange or reddish light, distant objects will show up in lighter shades of those colors.

Leonardo seems to have been the first painter to mimic this effect in his paintings. In the *Mona Lisa*, for example, he made the crags and forests in the background indistinct and greenish blue in hue, to give the painting a greater sense of depth. This was revolutionary in Leonardo's time, but it has become a standard device in representational art since then. It can also serve the garden designer well: to create an illusion of greater depth in a confined space, the designer can plant bluish and gray-foliaged plants at the back, or blue and purple flowers. These colors can make the plantings seem more distant than they actually are. To enhance the effect, the gardener may fill the foreground with brighter reds, oranges, and yellows, which through contrast make the blue, gray, and purple background seem even more remote.

SHADOW

> For most of us, shadows occupy the border of consciousness; the area where the real gives way to the imagined, where ghosts and half-remembered visions flourish. My interest in shadows lies in their ability to conjure up an added spatial dimension. They help clarify the ambiguities, which are inherent in visual perception, and they point to the crucial role which light plays in determining how we interpret events in the world around us. Most importantly, letting shadows take over the primary narrative role helps me open up the question of what is real.
>
> —SCULPTOR LARRY KAGAN

If light is often poorly understood by gardeners, shadow is something almost entirely ignored. We include areas of shade as a refuge from the summer sun, but otherwise let the shadows (like the chips) fall where they may.

Shadow is just an absence of light, and yet in its own way it has an equal or greater impact. It is the shadows, after all, that reveal and even emphasize the surface textures of objects—the craters of the moon are made visible not by the light this heavenly body reflects, but by the moon's darker, unreflecting areas. Shadows are also what let us read visually the volume of objects. This was another fact recognized by that versatile genius Leonardo, who in paintings such as *The Adoration of the Magi* brought to perfection the technique now known as *chiaroscuro*. Using a skillful gradation of darker tones to suggest shadows, the artist endowed the two-dimensional figures and objects he painted with an apparent third dimension, or mass.

Of more importance to gardeners is another technique that Leonardo used. He put it this way:

I would remind you O Painter! To dress your figures in the lightest colors you can, since, if you put them in dark colors, they will be in too slight relief and inconspicuous from a distance. And this is because the shadows of all objects are dark. And if you make a dress dark there is little variety between the lights and shadows, while in light colors there will be greater variety.

In other words, he suggested that by creating a backdrop of shadows, painters—designers—can highlight and emphasize those objects within a composition that they consider central. Set a reflective, bright-foliaged shrub or a gleaming marble or steel sculpture in front of a background of some less reflective material such as an evergreen hedge heavily patterned with shadow, and the effect is like that of a well-aimed spotlight. The eye is drawn irresistibly to the light.

A GARDEN IN GEORGETOWN

Though the bold sweeps of perennials and grasses popularly dubbed "the New American Garden" have become a signature of our firm, our style (like that of any skilled designers) adapts to suit circumstances and clients' tastes. This is particularly apparent in the many compact urban oases we have created for clients' townhouses. These gardens are necessarily on a very different scale than those we create for suburban or rural landscapes, and typically feature a different palette of plants and effects. To harmonize with the man-made character of the setting, our city gardens frequently put more emphasis on the "hardscape," the built elements. Because clients are usually seeking a retreat from the noise and confusion of city life, our urban designs also tend to be more introverted in mood. Surrounded by buildings and—in older residential neighborhoods—by street trees, our city gardens are frequently shady ones. In these circumstances, the play of light and shadow becomes an even more important design effect.

This is certainly the case in a garden in Washington's historic Georgetown neighborhood that we redesigned in 2007–2008 for a Venezuelan couple. I say "redesigned" because this was one of those most flattering commissions: an encore. We

THE NEWLY ADDED TERRACE WITH STRINGERS OF RED BRICK AND A FIELD OF LIMESTONE. THE POOL HOUSE IS TO THE RIGHT AND THE MAIN HOUSE TO THE LEFT.

had designed the existing garden for the house's previous owners back in the early 1980s. The garden had aged well, on the whole, but the new owners' different tastes and needs made an update desirable. When the new owners contacted us, we accepted the challenge of reinterpreting the site.

The difference in the lifestyles of the two sets of owners was fundamental. Whereas the previous owners had been raising children in the house, the new owners' children were grown and on their own. A lawn on which their children could play and picnic had been essential to the first couple; the second couple, who are socially active, wanted more space for outdoor entertaining. In any event, the lawn was in decline. The trees we had planted in the garden in the 1980s had grown up, and so had the trees

THE ORIGINAL TERRACE WITH STRINGERS OF LIMESTONE AND A FIELD OF RED BRICK.

in neighbors' yards and on the adjoining streets (the house is set on a corner lot). There was no longer enough direct sunlight reaching the garden floor to support healthy turf.

The decision to sacrifice the lawn, then, was an easy one. The garden occupies an L-shaped site between the house and a pool house, with the vertical back of the L running north and south. A swimming pool and fountain occupied most of the L's foot. Along its northern edge we had set a terrace of red brick panels bordered with pale limestone stringers. Turf occupied the remaining space, approximately one-third of the whole. This we removed in our redesign, replacing it with a continuation of the terrace, though the new pavement exactly reversed the proportions of limestone and brick in the old. Thus, in the new area that we created as an outdoor dining room, panels of tawny limestone slabs are bordered by thin bands of red brick. A simple device, the reversal in the pavement served to set the dining area apart from the original poolside terrace. By visually dividing the space, the transition from one pavement to another also warded off a sense of monotony that might otherwise have resulted from such a heavily architectural treatment of the space.

Traditional design wisdom is that in dealing with small, enclosed spaces such as this, you should keep the various elements within it compact, supposedly to make the space seem larger. In fact, what we have found at our firm is that such practice only leads to an impression of meagerness. We avoid clutter by limiting the plants and furnishings, but what we do include we ensure is bold and generous in scale. The dining terrace, for example, ordinarily features only a single round table and four armchairs, although it can at need accommodate enough tables and chairs to seat fifty diners. Likewise, in replacing older, sun-loving plantings such as feather reed grass (*Calamagrostis acutiflora* 'Stricta') we stuck to bold-foliaged plants such as hostas, or swaths of smaller-leaved plants such as

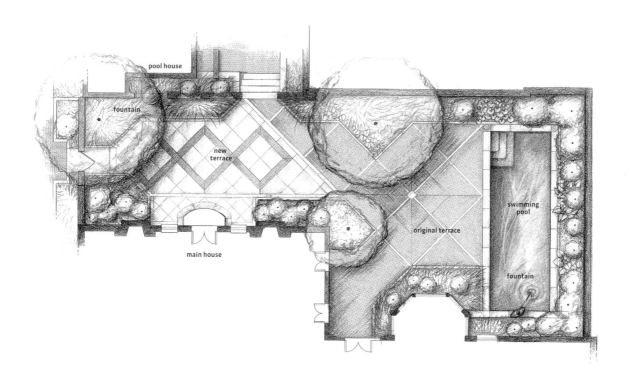

pool house

fountain

new
terrace

swimming
pool

original terrace

main house

fountain

the glossy-foliaged (and evergreen) European ginger (*Asarum europaeum*). The new plants are not only better adapted to shade, but more assertive visually.

By setting the lines of the pool and terraces at different angles, we had energized the site; this simple but dynamic pattern proved a wonderful setting for the play of light and shadow that projects down through the overhanging trees. As the sun moves across the sky, this natural calligraphy constantly changes. We had dressed the tall brick wall that encloses the garden with niches and half columns for the previous owners; in early morning and late afternoon now, beams of raking light penetrate to spotlight these details. We maximized the light every way we could. By painting the interior of the swimming pool with an ultramarine paint, we turned its surface into a mirror to reflect both sun and the surrounding scenes. The plants, spilling over edges and climbing toward the sun, soften the edges of the masonry and interrupt the planes, ensuring that our collage of shadow and light doesn't become forbiddingly stark.

UNDERSTANDING SHADOW THROUGH PHOTOGRAPHY

On the wall of my living room hangs a photograph I particularly prize, one that is also extraordinarily relevant to the subject of this chapter. It is a black-and-white portrait of the artist Henri Matisse in his studio, taken by one of the greatest masters of shadow in the history of photography, the Hungarian-born artist who called himself simply "Brassaï."

Awareness of shadow is central to the photographer's art. In addition to giving depth to form, shadow defines visual patterns, creating rhythms, contrast, and drama in photographs. It also serves as a means of manipulating mood; the intrinsic emotional overtones of such words as "gloomy," "bright," "beaming," and "dim" indicate how effective this can be.

An understanding or the use of shadow, then, is stock in trade for any photographer, especially one who chooses to work in black-and-white, eliminating the world of color. It's no accident that the definitive self-portrait of Ansel Adams, the great black-and-white photographer of our western landscape, is a view of his own shadow projected onto a rock.

But Brassaï's use of shadow stands out even in this company. A fugitive from the collapse of the Austro-Hungarian empire, he settled in Paris in 1924. His interest in photography was initially almost an accident. He had spent several years living hand to mouth, working as a freelance journalist to support his real interest, which was an obsessive exploration of Parisian nightlife in all its extremes of glamour and squalor. Trained as a painter, Brassaï turned to photography to document his nocturnal adventures, and he made his reputation in 1933 with the publication of *Paris After Dark*, a volume of sixty-four disturbing black-and-white masterpieces.

The interest of these photographs from the gardener's perspective is the powerful use Brassaï makes of shadow. His equipment was primitive even for the era in which he worked: a tripod-mounted folding camera with a lens mounted at the end of a long bellows and, for supplementary light when necessary, magnesium flash powder. Long exposures—he'd leave the lens unshuttered for the length of time it took him to smoke a cigarette—often allowed Brassaï to make do with the illumination of the city streetlights alone.

The results were alternately elegant and sinister. Thus, in a view shot down a path of the Luxembourg Gardens, shadows from the railings criss-cross like the cross-hatched lines of an antique engraving, framing the pale statue of a nymph that glows atop a pedestal. In a view shot almost at ground level down an empty street, shadow emphasizes the texture of the cobblestones, turning pavement into a modernist abstract. In these photographs, objects emerge from the dark: the cone-shaped flower clusters of a horse chestnut gleam in the darkness like chandeliers. Lack of light reduces objects and people to silhouettes, lending an air of mystery to what by daylight would likely be too obvious and pedestrian to deserve a second glance.

Available in a reprinted version published in 1987, *Paris After Dark* is well worth a look, even though it may take some time for your local library to locate a copy.

I know of only one similarly explicit use of shadow by a gardener. While reshaping an East Hampton estate for a tree-infatuated client, New York landscape architect Douglas Reed not only planted a host of new specimens while grooming the existing trees, he also pruned the limbs that overhung the lawn so that they would cast more striking patterns onto the turf.

This effect may be too esoteric for you. That's fine. But don't neglect the use you can make of a backdrop of shadows to dramatize some brightly colored garden feature. Twist the end of a path into the dim obscurity of a stand of tall shrubs or trees to add an element of mystery. Place a rugged boulder in a sun-drenched spot where its roughly shadowed surface will contrast with the finer textures of enclosing herbs—rosemary and thyme, sage and oregano. Be aware of the light in your garden and use to the fullest all the shadows, colors, and textures it creates.

SCULPTOR
ROBERT ADZEMA

Robert Adzema is an artist who works in an uncommon medium: he sculpts sunlight. That is, he creates sundials. But his are not of the clichéd garden-ornament "I count only sunny hours" type. Rather, each one is unique, a study and expression of how sun, earth, and time interact at a particular point in space. Robert's sundials are instruments of power, in the direct tradition of those with which Neolithic priests marked the passage of seasons at Stonehenge.

Robert still remembers a moment from childhood when he paused to look at dust motes floating in the ray of sunshine slipping in through a Venetian blind. He recalls how he felt a sudden wonder at the way those insubstantial specks transformed what had been an intangible beam, pure energy, into something with a physical presence.

That vision was in the back of his mind when, a couple of decades later, a New York City university commissioned him to create a piece for its campus plaza. The university administrators expected a clock tower. After some thought, Robert decided to give his clients a less conventional timepiece, one that truly marked the spot. So he designed for the university his first sundial.

The administrators failed to share Robert's vision, and that project never got built. Nevertheless, this experience changed Robert's art. He became absorbed by the specificity of sundials. To function accurately, each one must be designed for the sunlight that strikes a particular site. Indeed, what makes a sundial work is its mimicry of the motions and relationships of earth and sun. The dial as a whole must be aligned with our planet's geographical north pole, and the gnomon—the part that casts the shadow—must precisely parallel the axis on which the earth rotates. If these elements are correct, the dial becomes an instrument for reading accurately the daily rotation of the earth with respect to the sun and so the progression of the hours.

Sundials can be highly accurate timepieces—some French railway

station masters continued to use "heliochronometers" to set their clocks, the ones that regulated the schedules of the trains, until 1900. But with a bit of imagination the maker can persuade the dial to tell far more than just hours, minutes, and seconds. A sundial can be more accurate than a compass in revealing the direction of true north. It locates Polaris, the North Star; and in fact the world's largest sundial, a 90-foot-tall monster in Jaipur, India, was built as an astronomical instrument. It can also measure the progression of time over the seasons, as Robert Adzema demonstrated in a dial he created on the roof of a Brooklyn elementary school. Because the axis of the earth is tilted with respect to the sun, the angle at which sunlight strikes each part of the earth changes continuously (and cyclically) over the course of the earth's annual orbit around that star. This not only causes the seasonal changes in local climates, but also ensures that the tip of a gnomon's shadow hits the face of the sundial at a slightly different spot each day at noon. By marking those spots and labeling each with a month and day, Robert turned the school's dial into a solar-powered calendar.

Robert tells of what must be the most ingenious use of sundials, one

ROBERT ADZEMA,
SUNDIAL, 1980.
BRONZE.
Private collection.

practiced by the ancient Greek scholar Eratosthenes. More than two hundred years before the birth of Christ, Eratosthenes set up two sundials 5,000 stadia (roughly 500 miles) apart and then measured the angle at which the sun struck each dial precisely at noon on the same day. By measuring the difference between the two angles, Eratosthenes, a skilled mathematician, was able to calculate what fraction of the distance around the earth the interval between the dials represented, and so estimate the circumference of the earth. Scholars disagree about the exact length of the unit Eratosthenes used to measure distances. Depending on which argument you accept, the error of Eratosthenes' estimate of the earth's circumference was no more than 16.3 percent (an impressive achievement considering the simplicity of his instruments) and perhaps as little as 1 percent. Robert's own sundials emphasize the beauty of the instruments as much as their functional value. Just a short walk from his studio, in the university campus next door, one floats like an abstract bronze swan in the middle of a lily pond. It's a collective memorial for seven children whose lives were cut short in separate incidents. It functions as a timepiece, marking every day the hours those children never lived to see. But Robert also pierced this sculpture with a meticulously routed hole. At noon on each child's birthday, if the day is sunny, the beam that focuses through the hole passes over a mirrored bead set in a shadowed part of the dial, kindling, for just a moment, a point of blazing light.

Made of wood and stainless steel, stone and ceramic, even paper, as well as bronze, Robert's sundials range from monumental pieces a dozen feet tall to assemble-yourself models a few inches across. What they all share is a clean, functional simplicity. The one at the Brooklyn school, for example, a glittering tile mosaic, depends on the child to serve as gnomon—when he or she stands at a marked spot, it is the child's shadow that tells the time and the date. The exact arrangement of the curves, lines, angles, and holes in each is dictated in part by astronomical calculations. They also exhibit a harmony reflecting that of nature.

When asked, the artist gladly steps outdoors to reveal the secret of reading the sun. All you have to do, he says, is do as his dials do: look and take notice.

To demonstrate, Robert aligns himself so that like one of his dials he faces due south. He judges the direction by the sun and, when checked with a compass, his orientation proves more accurate, since the compass points to a magnetic pole rather than a geographic one.

Robert directs himself this way, he explains, because in North America the sun's apparent path (it is of course really the earth and not the sun that moves) stays in the southern half of the sky. The sun crosses every day from the eastern horizon to the west. Its arc stays lowest, closest to the horizon, at the winter solstice (December 22) and gradually moves higher in the sky until noon of the summer solstice (June 21). After that, it begins to subside back toward that southern horizon. You doubtless have learned this in science class, but a sundial maker knows it through observation.

For a gardener, these changes in the sun's apparent path determine what will and won't be in the sunshine at different times of day in different seasons.

Stand beside Robert and imagine what this means. That large evergreen—Robert points ahead and to the left (he is still facing south)—will block the morning light from falling on the spot where he stands until about May, when the sun's path will have risen high enough in the sky to clear the tree's top. That oak directly to his right (due west) will block the late afternoon sun in mid-summer, but not in spring and fall, when the sun passes below the screen of its branches.

After spending time with Robert Adzema's sculptures, gardeners see the sun, and how it illuminates their landscapes, with new understanding. You become grounded in a powerful way, conscious of your intersection of earth and heavens. So, too, does a sundial ground the landscape. Facing intently north to read the light, this astronomical mimic creates an axis, invisible but palpable within the garden. Like those dust motes floating in the sunbeam, a sundial makes visible the sun.

MAKING THE SCENE
The Painterly Approach
to Garden Design

3

When the eye is trained to perceive pictorial effect, it is frequently struck by something—some combination of grouping, lighting and colour—that is seen to have that complete aspect of unity and beauty that to the artist's eye forms a picture. Such are the impressions that the artist-gardener endeavours to produce in every portion of the garden.

—GERTRUDE JEKYLL,
COLOUR SCHEMES FOR
THE FLOWER GARDEN

A FIELD OF FLOWERS
AND GRASSES ON
EVENING ISLAND AT
THE CHICAGO BOTANIC
GARDEN IN GLENCOE,
ILLINOIS.

I mentioned in the introduction to this book that I began my study of landscape with a brush rather than a spade. Thanks to the encouragement of an artistically inclined neighbor, I spent many hours as a teenager out in the Michigan countryside, trying to capture in paints the scenes I saw before me. This is a very useful practice for any gardener, be-

cause transcribing a scene onto canvas or paper requires that you first decide what details or qualities determine the character of that particular landscape. Is it the topography, the arrangement of hill and slope, the sweep of the horizon, or the enclosure of surrounding peaks that speaks to you? Or is it the lushness of the foliage contrasting with rugged stone outcrops, the brilliant scattering of floral colors over a meadow, the drama of water plunging over a falls? Identify the characteristic features that stir and attract you, and you begin to develop a design vocabulary that you can use to express yourself in your own landscape.

I urge you to try this. Take a sketchbook and pencil or watercolor paints to some favorite outdoor spot and try to capture what you see there. Don't let your hand's lack of skill discourage you. The point isn't the image you create, but rather the observation that goes into the act of transcription. In fact, a sketch or painting that disappoints you can be as informative as one you feel is a success: Compare the failed attempt with the scene that surrounds you and try to analyze what it is that your sketch is lacking. What did you miss?

You can also approach this process from the opposite direction. That is, you find what stirs or pleases you in paintings and then apply that to the landscape. It has in fact been a long time since I did any sketching from nature. But I enjoy visiting museums and galleries, and often I notice details in paintings, or uses of color, or techniques of composition that intrigue me. These things stick in my mind, and I find them occurring to me when I work on landscape designs.

For example, I have found the paintings of seventeenth-century Dutch masters such as Pieter de Hooch and Jan Vermeer to be rich sources of inspiration for pavements. To use such great art in such a pedestrian way may seem almost comically anticlimactic, but the fact is that these men lived and worked in an era when the Netherlands was at the peak of

ANNE TRUITT (1921–2004), *UNTITLED,* 1978. ACRYLIC ON CANVAS, 60" X 60". Private Collection.

its wealth, when it was the cosmopolitan center of Europe, and it was a golden age for architecture as well as art. In works such as De Hooch's *The Courtyard of a House in Delft* and *The Linen Closet* or Vermeer's *The Music Lesson* I've found elegant examples of tile, brick, and stonework, with patterns that have often inspired me as I was designing pavements for clients' terraces (and surely it is no coincidence that De Hooch's father was a bricklayer).

More often the inspiration I find in a painting is not so literal. I de-

scribed in the introduction how a Helen Frankenthaler painting, *Nature Abhors a Vacuum,* helped me communicate to a client the use of color and style I envisioned for her project. Likewise, one of the inspirations I drew on when I designed the garden surrounding my own weekend house (a project I'll describe in greater detail in the next chapter) was a painting by the twentieth-century artist Anne Truitt.

I became aware of Truitt's work through visits to Washington's Pyramid Galleries back in the 1970s. In 1977 I purchased one of her paintings. This is an expansive but not monumental work, a 5-foot-by-5-foot square of stretched canvas, painted, for the most part, white. Not a blank white, though. Across the bottom, like a horizon, runs a quarter-inch-wide stripe of lavender, and above that a thin line of red, and above that, about an inch up, two horizontal bands where Truitt applied the white paint more thickly so that although the color matches the background, the bands stand out in relief.

Truitt has only recently, and posthumously, been accorded recognition as having been among the first rank of post–World War II American artists. I feel a connection to her work because she, too, chose to live in Washington and because of her ties to the Eastern Shore of the Chesapeake Bay, an area I love and where I built my weekend retreat. Truitt was born and lived until she was thirteen in the little town of Easton, Maryland; my house is in the village of Sherwood, only ten miles away.

Truitt interests me because although she concentrated for the most part on sculpture, she was fascinated by how form interacts with color. Her sculptures most often resolved themselves into simple rectilinear wooden constructions that Truitt painted with multilayered, cross-hatched glazes of hand-brushed color. In a volume of her memoirs, *Daybook: The Journal of an Artist,* Truitt described these works as an at-

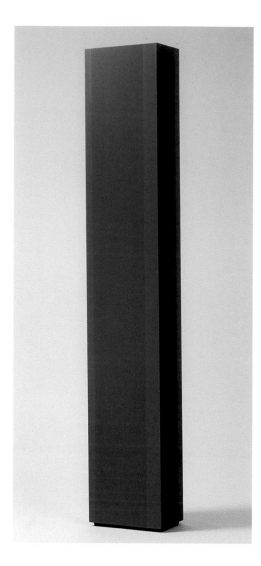

tempt "to take paintings off the wall, to set color free in three dimensions for its own sake." This is a fair description of one of the aspects of my own craft that most fascinates me.

Truitt was, both personally and artistically, extremely sensitive to the landscape. She chose to make her home in Washington because, she said, "The light is wonderful in Washington. . . . It's the latitude and longitude I was born on." In *Daybook* she admitted that she had never felt comfortable during a three-year stint in Tokyo because the light was so unfamiliar. She also refers several times to how strongly her artistic consciousness was marked by memories of the Eastern Shore's horizontal landscape—the line of fields meeting sea or sky, a setting in which trees, buildings, even people appear as vertical punctuation. She compares it to the landscapes of the Netherlands, the home of my ancestors and a place where I spent formative years as a young man. I always tell people that mountains may be magnificent, but they make me feel claustrophobic. Surely this is why I feel so in sympathy with the open and horizontal composition of the Truitt painting I am so fortunate to own. It's also why, I'm sure, the painting seems so at home in my house on the seashore.

When my father, a matter-of-fact Dutch Calvinist, first saw this pale, subtle painting hanging on the wall of my house, he asked me if it was where I projected photographic slides. "That would work," I told him. Which was true: the landscape that inspired Truitt is an expanse in which the challenge is to frame views. I've gradually realized this as my St. Michaels garden matures. When I first planted it, I was so careful not to interrupt the sweeping vista. Gradually, though, I've let a select few of the juniper trees that invaded the meadow along the shore grow up, to interrupt the horizontal and direct the eye.

PAINTING A PICTURE IN THE LANDSCAPE

> All gardening is landscape painting.
>
> —Alexander Pope

The deliberate framing of views is a tool that's essential to both the painter's and the garden designer's crafts, and its use is one that gardeners learned from painters. The style of landscaping that evolved into the classic English garden first began to emerge in the eighteenth century, inspired by paintings aristocratic youths brought home from the tour of Italy that was then the capstone of an upper-class education. In the preceding century, two French artists who emigrated to Rome, Claude Lorrain and Nicolas Poussin, had discovered the beauties of the Italian countryside and had, for almost the first time in European art, made the landscape the focus of painting instead of just a backdrop to human or divine figures. In particular, Lorrain's romantic pastorals of Roman ruins set amid gnarled trees, crags, and lush meadows became particularly popular as souvenirs for traveling English lordlings, who tried to reproduce these scenes on their own estates when they returned home.

The profession that arose to serve these men—represented by the pioneers of English garden design such as William Kent and Capability Brown—conceived of their landscapes largely as a series of views to be viewed from calculated perspectives along well-marked paths or carriage roads.

Conveniently, you don't have to fly to England to experience this style of design at first hand. What will probably

SCULPTOR HENRY MOORE'S
RECLINING FIGURE
IN THE DONALD M. KENDALL
SCULPTURE GARDENS
AT PEPSICO WORLD
HEADQUARTERS
IN PURCHASE, N.Y.

be the last great landscape of that tradition is the campus of the PepsiCo corporate headquarters in Purchase, New York. When the company settled on this 168-acre site in the early 1970s, Donald Kendall, a cofounder of the company, seized the opportunity to create a vast sculpture garden. He amassed a collection of some forty-five pieces by eminent artists such as Henry Moore, Alberto Giacometti, and Joan Miró and then hired the English landscape architect Russell Page to design the sculptures' setting. Page's previous clients had included the Duke and Duchess of Windsor and King Léopold III of Belgium, and he conceived of the PepsiCo campus in much the same manner as an aristocratic park. Planting on a grand scale, and for the most part in the romantic English tradition, he threaded the landscape with a "Golden Path" that takes the visitor through a series of viewpoints, openings through the masses of trees and shrubs that are calculated to show the sculptures and other landscape features to best advantage. Though created for the benefit of PepsiCo employees, the garden is open to the public, and I urge you to experience this extraordinary cross-pollination of painting, sculpture, and the landscaper's art the next time you find yourself in the New York City area.

COMPOSITION

> Whether I am making a landscape or a garden or
> arranging a window-box I first address the problem
> as an artist composing a picture; my preoccupation is
> with the relationship between objects whether I am
> dealing with woods, fields or water, rocks or trees,
> shrubs and plants or groups of plants.
>
> —RUSSELL PAGE

For Russell Page, addressing the landscape as a painter would compose a picture was a natural impulse. He had studied painting at London's Slade School of Art; it was the only formal education he took with him when he set up as a landscape designer. This approach worked well for Page, especially in a commission such as the PepsiCo headquarters, where the garden was intended to be a series of tableaux. In most other situations, however, I would find such a look-but-don't-touch style of design too static and limiting. I like to immerse myself in a garden, to wander and experience at will, and I grow impatient if it offers only prescribed experiences. Anyway, most of us want to be more than observers in our own space. When we work for private clients, my firm more typically conceives of the garden as an extension of their daily lives, a setting that supports and enhances all their activities.

THE PEPCO GREEN ROOF CREATES DRAMATIC VIEWS FOR THE APARTMENTS THAT WRAP AROUND IT AT THE WATER STREET APARTMENT COMPLEX IN WASHINGTON, D.C.

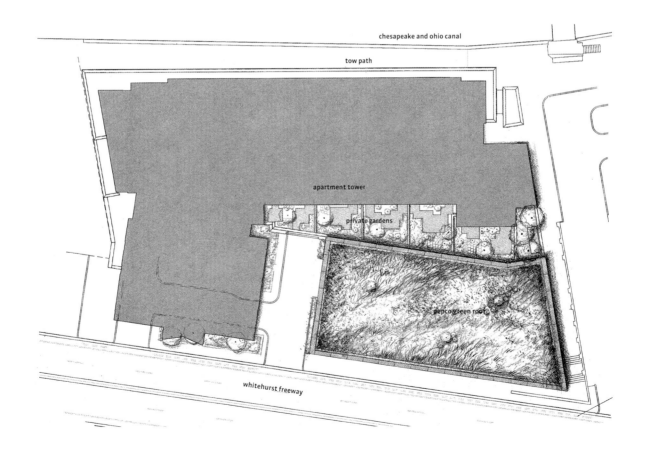

chesapeake and ohio canal

tow path

apartment tower

private gardens

pepco green roof

whitehurst freeway

Nevertheless, views do play an important role in most of our designs, even if it is just the view from the house into an urban court, and it is very useful to do what Russell Page did and study how painters address composition.

The first and most important point is to decide what will be the visual focus of the garden-picture (and keep in mind that a garden of any size will present a succession of such pictures). What features, either existing or to be created, will be the nucleus around which you build your design?

In an urban oasis (see pages 36–53

ABOVE: **VIEW FROM A WATER STREET APARTMENT OVER THE PEPCO ROOF TOWARD ROSSLYN, VIRGINIA.**

VIEW ACROSS THE PEPCO ROOF TOWARD THE KEY BRIDGE THAT CROSSES THE POTOMAC RIVER IN GEORGETOWN.

for photographs) that my partner Sheila Brady designed and installed for
another couple in Washington's Georgetown neighborhood (the firm has
done a lot of work in this vicinity), the views were introspective. This was
actually an update of a garden we designed for the property's previous
owners; when the house changed hands in 2002, the new owners came to
us to have the landscape refreshed.

THE GREEN ROOF OVER
THE PEPCO ELECTRICAL
POWER STATION INSPIRED
BY A PAINTING BY HELEN
FRANKENTHALER.

ABOVE: VIEW FROM THE
KITCHEN TERRACE TOWARD
THE MAIN TERRACE AND
FOUNTAIN. THE STUDIO IS
ON THE LEFT.

THE MAIN TERRACE
WITH THE FOUNTAIN.

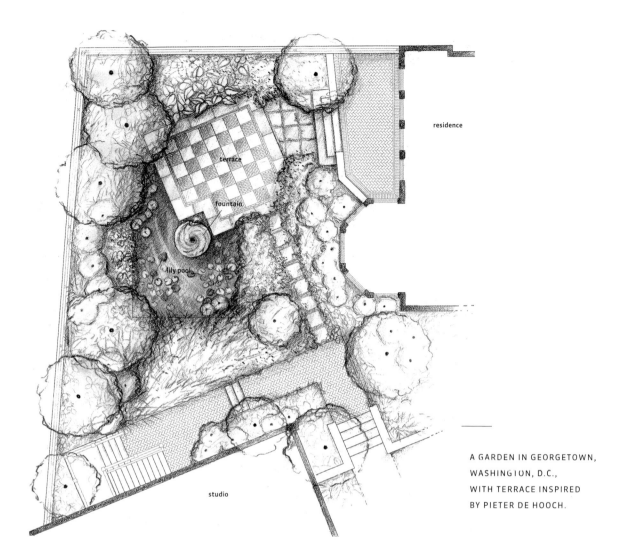

residence

terrace

fountain

lily pool

studio

A GARDEN IN GEORGETOWN,
WASHINGTON, D.C.,
WITH TERRACE INSPIRED
BY PIETER DE HOOCH.

The topography was challenging. The site is sloping, and we had to step the garden down through a succession of terraces: a narrow terrace accessible from the clients' kitchen is linked by stairs to a more expansive central terrace, and then through more stairs to a lower terrace featuring a swimming pool. Because the goal was to provide an escape from the city, Sheila chose to draw the eye and attention inward. The brick wall that surrounds the garden was heightened by capping it with a linear trellis, a feature that enhances the impression of enclosure while still allowing the passage of light and air.

The garden presents a series of focal points and views, but it is unified by the use of the same architectural materials—cut bluestone flags and brick—throughout. The pool, obviously, is the heart of the lowest terrace. The double flight of stairs leading up to the central terrace turns sharply at a landing, which in turn revolves around a classical statue set on a spiraling columnar plinth. The terrace adjacent to the kitchen is nothing more than an extended landing, a vantage point from which to survey the heart of the garden, the central terrace. A larger and more complicated space with a number of functions—relaxing, entertaining, outdoor dining—the central terrace needed a really strong focal point to pull it together. This Sheila supplied with a limestone fountain, a stylized cross-section of a nautilus shell, that she designed herself.

This feature seizes the attention of both eye and ear with the sparkle and murmur of falling water. Sheila set the fountain not at the most obvious point, the literal center of this level of the garden but in-

THE LIMESTONE
FOUNTAIN IN THE SHAPE
OF A NAUTILUS SHELL.

stead at its functional and visual center, the place where the two strongest elements, the terrace and the lily pond, intersect. The square pedestal on which the fountain rests, though surrounded by water, is set into a niche cut out of a projecting corner of the terrace. The pedestal is not only in the exact shape of the cutout but is also made of the same stone as the terrace's border, so that it looks as if a giant hand grabbed the terrace corner and pulled it out into the pond. In this way the fountain links land and water, becoming the pivot around which the two revolve.

SYMMETRY

Symmetry is a powerful—sometimes too powerful—compositional tool. In its crudest sense, when a scene is arranged so that one half exactly reflects the other, it becomes a very blunt instrument. This arrangement does create an irresistible visual axis at the meeting of the two halves, an axis that pulls every viewer's eye immediately down the same central line. The correspondence—the fact that each object on one side is matched by a twin on the other—also creates a powerful sense of control. In the princely gardens of Renaissance Europe, such simple symmetry became a means of expressing power, a visual symbol of the owner's ability to tame even nature.

Few of us aspire to that sort of grandiosity today. Besides, a landscape with such an obvious and predictable composition is boring. Applied in smaller doses, however, and more sensitively, symmetry can be very useful. The pavements I admired in classic Dutch paintings, for example, are strictly symmetrical in pattern, serving as a foil for the asymmetric, organic forms of the human figures who are the paintings' focus. We echoed those pavements in the checkerboard of pink brick and gray bluestone with which we surfaced the central terrace of the garden described above.

The symmetry of the masonry's pattern accentuates the irregular luxuriance of the surrounding plantings. Furthermore, by rotating the terrace slightly, aligning it at a slight but obvious angle from the wall that surrounds the garden and from the house, we were able to pit one symmetry, that of the terrace, against those of the architectural elements, injecting tension and energy into our composition.

Although this garden as a whole is certainly asymmetrical, the composition has what painters would call *balance*. That is, the weight and presence of the various elements are sufficiently similar that no single element overwhelms the others. Pool, planted areas, and terrace are all generously proportioned and of about the same scale, so that each serves as a counterpoise to the others. By adjusting the balance, as in this instance where we made the pool somewhat smaller than the terrace, the gardener can emphasize one element or another.

THE USE OF LINE

Anyone who has taken even the most casual interest in painting quickly learns the power of *line*. Line can be explicit, as in my Anne Truitt painting, or in the line of a wall or the horizon or the mast of a ship. But line can also be implied, as in the line suggested by Washington's steely look forward as he stands erect in the boat in Emanuel Gottlieb Leutze's famous painting *Washington Crossing the Delaware*. Painters use these lines to direct the viewer's eye; we have a tendency to follow the line to the places or objects at which they point, or to imagine how they intersect to frame a form or space.

In a similar way, the gardener can use line to connect a series of views and move the viewer through a landscape. In the garden described above, for example, the broad line of the brick and bluestone paving as it descends from the house and street into the terrace draws the eye to the center of the garden. The stone flags of the terrace, set corner to corner, imply diagonal lines that lead to the fountain.

To direct the eye to a view I want to emphasize, I'll often set a chair or a cluster of chairs in a prominent spot facing in the appropriate direction. I've found that passersby, when they notice the chairs, immediately check to see what it is they are arranged to view. I've even used sculpture for this purpose—people instinctively look to see what a statue is looking at.

Different sorts of lines—straight and sinuous, short and long, thick and fine—all lend a different feeling to a scene. I'll leave you to explore that yourself, but I urge you not to waste the opportunity that a line—the horizontal of a path or the edge of a bed, the vertical of a tree trunk or column—presents. Use them to frame the view or emphasize focal points. You may want to allow overspilling plants to soften the hard edge of masonry, but don't hide the line, and where it is visible, make it definite and crisp.

COLOR

Most gardeners, I find, are much more comfortable with this aspect of design than with composition. They know the colors they like, and they fill their gardens with these hues. Maybe the combinations run counter to accepted taste, but if it pleases you, so what? You shouldn't let anyone impose their preferences on you.

That, of course, is exactly what many popular gardening experts too often strive to do. Their articles, books, and television programs are rife with such prescriptive advice. Typically, this takes the form of recommendations for "plant partners" and "plant combinations." What they offer in these are recipes, complete with detailed lists of ingredients, that make it easy for you to achieve what the experts conceive of as an acceptable look. For me, this approach has no more appeal than those "paint by numbers" kits that were so popular in the 1950s. I always prefer originality and genuine self-expression in a garden, even if the taste is incompatible with my own.

This is not to say that all uses of colors are equal. Color is a tool, and the designer who understands it can greatly increase the impact of the scenes they construct. Be true to your own taste, in other words, but learn how to express it most effectively.

HARMONIES

Color has been the subject of intense study for centuries, attracting such profound thinkers as Leonardo da Vinci and Isaac Newton. Their observations and theories have become the foundation for an extensive science of color, complete with detailed analytic studies of the nature of color and how it is perceived by the human eye. The average gardener is likely to find this highly technical material difficult—and anyway, there's no need to explore it on your own. A long succession of painters, beginning with Leonardo, have spent lifetimes working out the practical aspects of how this science can translate into experience.

The most deliberately scientific of these painters were the Impressionists of the late nineteenth and early twentieth century. Many of them had studied the theories of Michel Eugène Chevreul, a chemist employed by the Gobelin tapestry works, whose *Principles of Harmony and Contrast of Colors* (published in 1839) was the leading study of the time. The great German essayist and poet Johann Wolfgang von Goethe had published a 1,400-page analysis of color and its perception three decades previously, in 1810, and this proved an equally formative text for the greatest landscape painter of the nineteenth century, J.M.W. Turner.

If you wonder what Turner can teach you, you have only to study the work of a young disciple of the following generation, a painfully near-sighted young woman named Gertrude Jekyll. Despite growing recognition of her work, Jekyll had to give up painting because the close work it involved was straining her eyes and exacerbating her myopia. She turned to garden design, and by applying what she had learned from studying and copying Turner's paintings (Jekyll never actually met the master, who died when she was eight years old), she revolutionized the field.

Jekyll has been hailed as sort of gardening deity, and she was an immensely knowledgeable horticulturist. Yet if you look at contemporary photographs of her gardens (Jekyll took many of these herself, for she was also an enthusiastic and technically accomplished photographer), you may wonder how she achieved success as a designer. That's because Jekyll and her contemporaries shot in black-and-white. What such photographs preserve are form and perspective, the basics of composition, and Jekyll clearly had a relatively weak grasp of that. Where she excelled was in an area that those photographs didn't preserve. She had an extraordinarily sensitive eye for color, one that had been refined in her study of Turner's paintings.

Jekyll studied and memorized the precise hue of thousands of flowers and foliages, and she used these as her palette in creating sophisticated, delicate color harmonies. She liked to explore all the tones and intensities of a particular hue and color, contrasting them with related colors. A border of mixed annual and perennial flowers (Jekyll's specialty) might progress from pink to rose, salmon, and intense reds, the flowers interspersed with dark reddish-purple foliages such as ajuga and oxalis. And though Jekyll let the flowers knit together in what she considered a more natural manner, she was careful to plant in sizable clusters or "drifts" of each cultivar so that the hues remained distinct.

FOLLOWING PAGES:
THE DUTCH GARDEN AT
HESTERCOMBE GARDEN,
SOMERSET, UNITED KINGDOM,
DESIGNED BY
GERTRUDE JEKYLL AND
SIR EDWIN LUTYENS.

OPPOSITE: SHORELINE PLANT-
ING IN THE GREAT BASIN AT
CHICAGO BOTANIC GARDEN.

ABOVE: THE SERPENTINE
BRIDGE CONNECTING EVENING
ISLAND TO THE MAIN ISLAND
AT CHICAGO BOTANIC GARDEN.

LEFT: VIEW OF THE GREAT
BASIN FROM THE SERPENTINE
BRIDGE IN WINTER.

Jekyll liked to mix blues in among cream whites and pale yellows; purple and lilacs she grouped together with pure whites and silver-gray foliages. She might run the whole spectrum in a single long border, but when she did, she took care to let the hues evolve through intermediate steps—blues, both light and dark, might intermix with pale yellow and white, which in turn could shade into pale pink, then rose, crimson, and scarlet, finishing in orange and bright yellow. To understand what she believed were nature's harmonies, Jekyll suggested that novices might study the blossom colors of different cultivars within some floral grouping such as a particular strain of azaleas or a race of irises. She was vociferous in her dislike of intense, bright colors, calling them "garish," praising the "true and delicate."

"The colours," Jekyll wrote in a magazine article, "should be placed with careful forethought and deliberation, as a painter employs them on his picture."

Interestingly, she was contemptuous of the " laws . . . laid down by chemists and decorators about colours which artists laugh at"; "to consider them," she added, "is a waste of time." Apparently, she was unaware of Turner's debt to the analysts.

CONTRASTS

There is no blue without yellow and without orange.

—Vincent van Gogh

Like any skilled colorist, Jekyll used contrasts between different hues to energize her compositions. Juxtaposing a drift of incandescent orange and a dark scarlet enhances both hues: as the eye moves from one to the other, the orange appears brighter and the scarlet richer and more intense. As a rule, though, she avoided the kind of bold contrasts that truly galvanize a painting or landscape. For examples of that more daring use of color, you do better to look at the paintings of Van Gogh.

What Van Gogh was alluding to in the quote at the beginning of this section is the extraordinary power of what are called *complementary contrasts*. This refers to a fact that artists and scientists had both noticed about color: that certain hues clash visually when set next to each other. Instead of blending visually, as related hues (an orange and a yellow) would do, the *complementary* ones seem to emphasize their difference. These complementary pairs include blue and orange, violet and yellow, and red and green. The Impressionist painters of nineteenth-century

VINCENT VAN GOGH,
*LE CAFÉ DE NUIT
(THE NIGHT CAFÉ),* 1888.
OIL ON CANVAS, 28.5" X 36.3".
Yale University Art Gallery.
Bequest of Stephen Carlton
Clark, B.A., 1903.

France didn't understand the physiological reasons for this effect, but they were aware of it, and they made use of the fact that when complementary colors are juxtaposed, they electrify a painting.

This is actually one of the secrets of the bold, almost manic energy you find in many of Van Gogh's masterpieces. In his self-portraits, for example, the terrifying intensity of the artist's eyes derives in large part from his use of such contrasts: in some, an orange beard is used to make the blue eyes jump out of the canvas, while in others, the eyes are green framed with strokes of red. Of *The Night Café,* in which he gave the sordid barroom a sinister glow through another use of complementary colors, he wrote, "I've tried to express the terrible human passions with the red and the green." And in his most famous painting, *The Starry Night,* Van Gogh made an orange and yellow moon and stars pulse, almost literally, by surrounding them with whorled brushstrokes of blue and violet.

DEVELOPING A PERSONAL
APPROACH TO COLOR

While I believe a gardener can learn much from the work of a master such as Van Gogh, it should be an inspiration, not a blueprint. The goal is to put the techniques to work in a way that enhances your own style. If we return for a moment to the Georgetown garden, you'll notice in the photographs some subtle color contrasts that have a Jekyllesque air: pale pink shrub roses intermingled with darker rose-colored blossoms, a planter of yellow pansies invigorating a backdrop of greenish PG hydrangea flowerheads. But we also used bolder, complementary contrasts: the blue of the bluestone pavers, for example, emphasizes the warm orange tones in the adjoining panels of brick, just as (after summer heat withered the pansies) salmon-hued geraniums embolden the clear blue heads of nearby mop-head hydrangeas.

One thing to keep in mind if you should be tempted to emulate too faithfully Gertrude Jekyll's intricate harmonies: she designed for a society in which skilled horticultural help came cheap. Her prodigal planting plans, which often included dozens of different species and cultivars in a single bed, depended for their success on a level of skilled labor that is unaffordable, and often unobtainable, today.

I've found that a smaller cast of self-sufficient perennials and grasses suits our clients better. Likewise, planting each kind of plant in larger sweeps and then allowing the different plants to spread and intermingle their hues (as in a Frankenthaler painting) leads to a less contrived look than Jekyll's highly orchestrated "drifts" while also simplifying maintenance. Because annuals burden clients with the task of seasonal replacement, I use them very sparingly. As the Georgetown garden described in this chapter illustrates, however, a planter of intensely colored, continuously blooming annuals can provide an invigorating point of contrast, not so different in its effect from those streaks of red with which Van Gogh framed a green eye.

ROBERT DASH
The Outdoor Exhibition

The only physical exercise [I get] outside of painting is gardening and I love it. It is a way of thinking out loud, actually about painting—proportion, mixture of things, changing. I mean it is very similar to painting. And it illustrates—the same thing with painting—the unlimited possibilities in a small area, because the garden is very small. I mean you can stunningly create the new composition by just slight movement or clipping, the same way you do in painting, wipe out, and so forth.

—ORAL HISTORY INTERVIEW
WITH ROBERT DASH,
SEPT. 22, 1974,
ARCHIVES OF AMERICAN ART,
SMITHSONIAN INSTITUTION

Robert Dash's paintings and lithographs hang in museums from Munich to Boston, Philadelphia, and Washington, and his studio in Sagaponack, New York, at the eastern tip of Long Island, continues to be a place of energy and experimentation. Yet he is arguably as famous for his work with a spade as with a brush or palette knife. Dash associated as a respected colleague with all the notable New York painters of the 1960s and '70s; he was particularly close to Willem de Kooning. His garden, however, which he named "Madoo"

(an old Scots word meaning "my dove"), has been a place of pilgrimage to everyone from Christopher Lloyd to Rosemary Verey—and myself.

The garden was born in the mid-1960s when Dash bought a tract of neglected farmland, just under two acres in all, complete with a pair of venerable but ramshackle barns and various outbuildings, all set at the edge of what were then potato fields. He didn't start with a plan for the garden, any more than he starts his paintings with a map. He just launched into digging and planting.

"Blunder!" he urges. "Get to the soil!" Just don't do anything indelible, not at first. Dash recommends spending at least a year walking and observing before you begin planting, and then create nothing immovable "until the garden is suggested to you."

As with a painting, the garden should be able to evolve as you work on it. Both gardening and painting, he adds, are "arts of the wrist"; in both you must be ruthless, willing to scrape the canvas or landscape bare if you recognize at some point that you've taken the composition down a wrong path.

Dash doesn't think of painting when he is gardening, or vice versa. Yet the one art clearly influences the other. Landscape—what he sees out of doors—has been a recurring theme in his painting, as have the flowers in his garden (though both often in a highly abstract form). Similarly, you would never mistake Madoo for anything other than a painter's garden. Dash uses the man-made structures in his garden to create points of visual contrast. You see his brushwork (literally) in the violet-colored gazebo, a trellis of glowing red edged with yellow, and a free-standing arch, little more than a curved line in chrome yellow, that perfectly frames a distant door of the exact same hue and shape.

The concept of "garden rooms" Dash feels is obsolete. It dates to an era when interior living space was divided into connected boxes, each with a separate function. Today, more of us, as Dash points out, tend to live in an open-plan house. The garden should follow suit. His does—the different experiences interconnect, more like a gallery exhibition of his work. A strong framework of green, much of it clipped to shape, provides structure.

The matching of texture, form, and color is sophisticated, but deliberately disconcerting. "If you are not breaking rules constantly," Dash insists, "you are not doing a good garden." When Dash wants more space, he conjures it. To create a vista without including the ugly buildings that have overrun the potato fields, Dash laid out a 120-foot-long brick-paved path with a rill of running water down the center, shaded by 12-foot-tall rose-clad arches. To lengthen the view, Dash employed a painterly trick of "forcing the perspective." That is, the end of the path nearest the house, and the arch over it, measure eight feet wide, but both path and arches narrow by regular increments, shrinking to a width of six feet at the far end. This fools the eye into perceiving the distance as greater than it actually is. And the trickery continues: the walk ends in a door that does not open, but that seems cut with a tall, thin plate of glass that appears to be a window looking out onto even more arbor and walk; in fact, it is a mirror.

More mirrors set into walls create more faux views into alternative realities. A bridge provides a viewing platform for sculpture, while a scattering of clipped boxwood globes (which Dash grew from cuttings) amid columnar trunks turns nature into abstraction. Dash has no illusion of who, ultimately, makes the decisions. An epidemic killed groves of black pines, an invasion of borers took almost all of his birches. Dash shrugged and adapted. When a hurricane fells a "precious tree" it can be hard, "but then you say, 'Oh, I like that space. That's beautiful. Why didn't I think of that?' "

A garden evolves, Dash explains; it becomes your autobiography and it alters you as you alter it. You have to remain open to opportunities. As De Kooning told him ("he was sitting right at this table," Dash says), "I have to change to remain the same."

This may be the most powerful message of Madoo, aside from its extreme sensory gratification: that a garden, like a painting, is an exploration. That you make your plans, but the master knows when to let go and let the work take on its own life.

4

RHYTHM AND MOVEMENT

How wrong are those simpletons, of whom the world is full, who look more at a green, a red, or similar high color than at the figures which show spirit and movement.

—MICHELANGELO BUONARROTI

It don't mean a thing
if it ain't got that swing.

—DUKE ELLINGTON

A CONNECTICUT
GARDEN. PATH FROM
THE HOUSE DOWN TO
THE LILY POOL AND
LOWER GARDEN. THE
STEPPING STONES ARE
INTERPLANTED WITH
HERBS.

It still makes me laugh whenever I reread the letter the late Roberto Burle Marx sent to me more than twenty years ago. "Have you ever thought," he asked, "that when you give someone a bouquet of flowers, you are giving them a bouquet of sexual organs?" I had not. But the query is characteristic of that freewheeling Brazilian genius, who spent more than six decades, from the early 1930s until his death in 1994, continuously reinventing the arts of landscape architecture and garden design.

These were not the only arts, nor even the first, in which Burle Marx excelled. He had studied piano and voice seriously as a youth, hoping to make music his career. His impromptu vocal performances at parties and celebrations—Burle Marx had a clear, fine, classically trained baritone—remained famous throughout his life. At age eighteen, he left Rio de Janeiro with his family to spend a year and a half in Berlin (his father was German-born), where he continued his music education and studied painting in the cultural ferment of the Weimar Republic. While searching for subjects to paint, he discovered a collection of Brazilian plants in Berlin's botanic garden. Seeing them in the foreign setting made him appreciate what he had left behind. He never abandoned music or painting (and he later worked in sculpture and a number of other media as well), but he returned to Brazil with a new appreciation of his native landscape and flora. A gardener since childhood, Burle Marx began to collect specimens of native plants, embarking on a series of expeditions to Brazil's forests and jungles. He eventually assembled a collection of 3,500 native species, a number of them previously unknown even to botanists, around his home in Barra de Guaratiba outside Rio.

When I went there to visit Burle Marx for three weeks in 1987, I found him concentrating on his painting, although he was also engaged in preparing for one of his storied parties (in this case, a Sunday lunch for two hundred), hand-painting tablecloths and building totem-pole-like sculptures of fresh fruits and flowers. All of these activities, as well as his work in jewelry and tapestry design and the sets and costumes he produced for theatrical productions, sprang from the same creative impulse and reflected the same vision. Although he defined himself as a painter, much of the vocabulary he used in his work on the landscape and elsewhere, his way of thinking about his art, clearly derived from his musical experience.

I touched on this aspect of Burle Marx's work briefly in a previous book (*Architecture in the Garden*), but because he was so fundamental a figure in the development of modern landscape architecture and the way we see gardens today, this topic deserves a more in-depth examination. I am struck now, as I was in 1987, at the bold and abstract way he used color. Indeed, Burle Marx used strong, simple hues in the landscape as a pianist might use the eight notes of the harmonic scale. That is, he rarely intermingled flowers of different colors, preferring instead to mass flowers or foliage of a single hue in a clearly defined expanse to enhance their cumulative impact—strike a clear tone—which he then played against notes of other colors in calculated harmonies and dissonances.

Burle Marx was also keenly aware of the role rhythms could play in the landscape as well as music. That was something I learned early, too. This author remembers from childhood his first meeting with a piano teacher. Gathering the fingers of my hand in hers, the teacher brought them down at random intervals on the keyboard. "That is noise," she said. Then she tapped with them in rhythm. "This is music."

In the same way, it is visual rhythms—the repetition of colors or forms, or even voids, at calculated intervals—that turn a landscape into a garden. Rhythm, really, is the heart of garden design. A garden's rhythm may be simple and explicit, as it is in the symmetrical geometry of the great French formal gardens. Equally, though, it may be subtle, even evanescent. The tasseled grasses of an Oehme, van Sweden garden, for example, bowing in succession to the wind, give these landscapes a different rhythm with every new breeze. Often, different areas of a garden will have distinct rhythms, and the distinction is likely to reflect different functions. A central path may be flanked at intervals by evergreen shrubs that

VIEW FROM A VIRGINIA
HOUSE OVER THE GARDEN
TOWARD THE RAPPAHANNOCK
RIVER.

establish a stately cadence, while the flower garden to which it takes you enjoys a livelier tempo set by a color or colors woven in asymmetrical patterns through the whole.

Burle Marx was a virtuoso in the creation of such visual rhythms, and his work was in this respect a great inspiration to me. He created rhythms even in lawns, often arranging two different-hued turfs in a carefully edged pattern, such as the staccato checkerboard of alternating squares he planted at the Olivo Gomes house in Sao Jose dos Campos (now preserved as a park), and the wavelike succession of sinuous bands he planted in Rio de Janeiro's Flamengo Park. He might space palms in a stately march across a vista, or array the immense, disk-shaped leaves of *Victoria amazonica* waterlilies in carefully disposed clusters in dramatic counterpoint to the zigzagging masonry edge of a pool. In many respects, Burle Marx's gardens were more a performance, a dance that changed with the light and seasons, than a static composition.

One of Burle Marx's greatest strengths as a designer was that he was instinctively in touch with the rhythms of the Brazilian landscape. A sensitivity to the regional rhythms is something that can be developed through observation, and it is something any gardener should cultivate. For if you draw a garden's rhythms from its surroundings, you relate the two to each other, giving your garden a sense of being rooted in the natural landscape.

You may find the rhythm in the general character or topography of the landscape: the sweep of a western plain, the crescendos and diminuendos of rolling hills, or the crashing chords of mountain peaks. Alternatively, you may find a rhythm in some more intimate feature of your immediate neighborhood or site. The rugged rhythm of natural rock outcroppings, for example, may serve as the organizing theme of your garden, or the staccato verticals of tree trunks in a woodland setting.

Rhythms may also be drawn from the house, of course. If the garden's views are aligned with windows, for example—a common and sensible practice—then the rhythm of the windows' placement within the architecture comes to dictate the layout of the landscape as a whole. At Oehme, van Sweden, we often integrate into the landscape rhythms drawn from the architecture, to achieve what we call "marrying" the house and garden, making the two function as a single unit. We may echo the stone of the house's walls in walls or pavements of the same material that we insert into the landscape, aligning the house and built features in a calculated pattern. If the lines of the house are simple, broad, and spreading, you may wish to echo that in an expansive, geometrical landscape. Of course, sometimes it's preferable to play against the rhythm of the archi-

tecture—a house that is too brutally rectilinear may need the softening effect of a gentler, curving rhythm in its landscape.

As you may gather from these reflections, my visit with Roberto Burle Marx changed my design life. Not in the sense that I tried to copy his work; the Brazilian master's style was not my style, and anyway, few of my clients would have opted for such abstract modernist designs. But the great scale on which he worked, both in the terms of the massing of plants and in sheer area (as in the 296-acre complex he created in a former landfill at Flamengo Park), I found thrilling. He had no fear. His use of color was so strong in comparison with the European and American traditions. And the earthy way he connected with the sensual side of his plants—since receiving that letter, I've never looked at a bouquet quite the same way ever again.

USING MUSIC IN YOUR DESIGN

> Jazz is there and gone. It happens. You have to be present for it. That simple.
>
> —KEITH JARRETT

Music, I would venture to guess, is the art to which most gardeners relate personally and on an ongoing basis. Many of us have some experience in making music ourselves, even if only in a school band or orchestra or singing at camp. In this age of the iPod, of course, we can create a whole soundtrack for our lives. Personally, I prefer to keep music as a special event rather than a constant background. Many designers, I know, listen to music as they work, and I have no doubt that the rhythms and themes entering their ears emerge in what comes from their fingers. This is actually why I do not listen as I design; I find the music too distracting.

But I think in musical terms often as I am creating a garden. Music

A GARDEN IN THE MOUNTAINS NEAR RIO DE JANEIRO DESIGNED BY ROBERTO BURLE MARX.

and its associated art, dance, are in many respects the ones I find to be closest to gardening. For gardening, like music and especially
dance, is a performance art, one that exists
only in the moment and leaves no permanent
fixed expression. That may seem a strange
simile to you, given that gardens can endure
for decades or even centuries. Yet because
they are composed of living things, they are
ever-changing. Flowers move in and out of
bloom, trees and shrubs grow and expand or
perhaps die, a sudden frost or storm trans-
forms a garden's appearance overnight. Every
day the garden re-creates itself; like Keith
Jarrett's jazz performance, it is there and
gone. You have to be present to experience it
in the moment.

In this respect, it helps to think of yourself as the conductor of the garden, trying to
make all the performers, the different plants,
work together while also recognizing that
each must express itself. To try to control
every aspect of the outcome will only rob the
performance of vitality. So, for example, I plan
carefully the plants I will use in a landscape
and where I will place them. But I enjoy the often unpredictable results, the different forms
the plants adopt through growth and the volunteer seedlings that may spring up as one

A GARDEN IN
BELGIUM DESIGNED
BY JACQUES WIRTZ.

species proves better adapted to the site than another. I try not to be too compulsive about weeding, removing only those plants that are clearly too aggressive or unsightly, and I advise clients to let the complex of plants within their gardens find its own balance.

I mentioned in the introduction to this book that thinking about the music you enjoy can provide a useful guide to the style with which you are comfortable. I listen to the Metropolitan Opera on the radio every Saturday, and it seems to me that the drama and the orchestral quality of that music is reflected in the sweep of my gardens and the calculated way in which the plants interact visually. Roberto Burle Marx was educated in the European classical tradition, but was also an enthusiastic promoter of Brazil's indigenous arts—in the jazzy, swinging sensuality of much of his work, I can feel the samba. My collaborator on this book, Tom Christopher, is trying to create a garden to suit a traditionally hewn timber-framed cottage he has built in the hills of western Massachusetts. He has sought inspiration in the contra dancing of that region, and says that (when he finally finishes the stone walls he is building) he will structure the landscape with groups of white birches interrelated like couples and foursomes in a contra dance "figure." We'll see.

My own enthusiasm when it comes to dance is ballet. I actually took classes at the Washington Ballet a couple of times a week for four years when I was in my forties. These were classes for adult members of the public; I had no illusions about my ability as a dancer, but I thought this experience would bring me a deeper understanding and appreciation of what happens onstage. This experience had a number of unanticipated benefits as well: it provided body-building exercise and gave me an improved physical presence and stance. In conjunction with the countless performances I've attended over the years, my ballet training greatly enhanced my understanding of how the human body moves.

However, any structured style of dance, from modern to ballroom, even square dancing, offers some of the same benefits. Above all, it will make you aware of choreography, which is an essential aspect of the garden designer's craft: just as in dance, the sequence in which you present the steps is fundamental to the experience as a whole. In other words, a garden shouldn't just present a chaotic grab bag of sensations; to be effective, you should present them in a calculated order. To open all the views of a garden to one vantage point, for instance, is to squander them—the visitor will take much more pleasure in discovering them one by one.

The most effective and least intrusive way to choreograph a garden experience is through the means of access you provide: the paths that take the visitor from spot to spot, and the barriers such as hedges, fences, or more informal screens that force the visitor to redirect and allow them forward only through certain gaps.

A skilled garden choreographer, however, can shape the experience at a far deeper level. You can, for example, use a twist in a path to turn the visitor suddenly toward a view; the turn will slow the steps and cause visitors to take notice of their surroundings. A landing halfway down a flight of steps can serve the same function, especially if you equip it with a bench. The easiest walking is on a path that follows the contours of a slope; turning the path so that it runs up or down the slope will slow the pace and cause the visitor to look down at where they set their feet. This can be a useful device to cause the visitor to notice a detail in the planting or distract them from an unattractive vista. Narrowing a path also slows walkers, encouraging a more contemplative pace and bringing them, literally, closer to their surroundings.

A CONVERSATION WITH LAWRENCE AND ANNA HALPRIN

The late Lawrence Halprin was one of the decisive figures in the history of American landscape architecture, the designer of such beloved public spaces as Ghirardelli Square in San Francisco and the Franklin Delano Roosevelt Memorial in Washington, D.C. He was married for more than sixty years to Anna Shuman Halprin, a giant in her own field, one of the pioneers of postmodern dance who is noted not only as a performer and teacher and the choreographer of 150 full-length dance theater works, but also for taking dance into new areas such as the treatment of the terminally ill and environmental education. Lawrence and Anna collaborated often in their work; with her help, Lawrence developed a technique he called "motation," a system of graphic notation to record how people move through space. I was able to speak to them about the role of choreography and dance in May 2006, a little more than three years before Lawrence's death at age ninety-three.

When I asked Lawrence about how his own work intersected Anna's, he explained that "in a sense, all my designs have to do with movement through space, and I think of the design of the landscape that way always, as places in which people move and have their being.

"It's about movement," he continued. "Everybody moves. The way you move and what you see and hear as you move affects the way you feel."

Anna jumped in: "There's a way of looking at movement and taking it out of the realm of dance, just looking at it from the realm of movement, which is universal to all people." The Halprins, I was learning, played doubles conversationally. "Everybody moves. Not everybody dances alike, but everybody moves and there are certain universal movements that evoke certain feelings. So that if . . . you create a design and everything is geometrical forms, in sharp corners, so when you move you move this way, this is going to affect the way you feel. But if you design in curves and things flow, [that] is going to affect the way you feel."

When I told Lawrence that I was contemplating the writing of this

book, that I was fascinated by the way that an interest in the other arts could influence work in our field, he said that this in fact had been an explicit element of his education as a landscape architect. A visit with Frank Lloyd Wright at Taliesin, his summer home in Wisconsin, had sparked Halprin's interest in this field and caused him to enroll in the Harvard Graduate School of Design. There he came under the direction of another giant of modern design, the German architect Walter Gropius, founder of the Bauhaus movement. As Lawrence recalled for me, "When I was at Harvard it was the high point of the Bauhaus period and they believed—Gropius actually believed—intensely about [the connection between design and the other arts]. And after all, he had dancers who taught in Bauhaus and he had designers. . . . I think of it all as a piece of theater, actually, where people who are designing are designing for things to happen."

Indeed, Lawrence, despite his horticultural background (which included a bachelor's degree in plant science from Cornell University and a master's degree in the same subject from the University of Wisconsin), rejected my use of the word "garden" in connection with the landscapes he had designed: "I don't even call them gardens, if you allow me to say that, because I don't think of this that we do as gardens. I think of them as spaces to be in."

A gardener may rebel at that rebranding, but it wasn't that Lawrence Halprin was insensitive to the natural elements in the landscape. As a younger man, he had been an avid hiker, spending much of his spare time exploring the high Sierra, and what he observed there, especially the tumbling waters, became a trademark of his urban design. It was no accident that when the National Park Service resolved to restore the approach to Yosemite Falls to a more natural state in 1995, it was Halprin they hired to develop a design. His plan removed a huge parking lot and other architectural elements and redesigned the trails. "The Park Service," he recalled, "wanted to modernize [the trails] and make them easier for visitors to move around. I wanted to blend them into the park better and make them less obvious. I thought, 'When I'm finished, I hope that no one knows I was here.'"

That is not only a humble but also an ambitious goal for any gardener. To recognize the natural potential of a site, and then to realize it so fully in your work that the result seems as if it has never been touched by human hands—that is artistry of the highest level.

A GARDEN IN
GREENWICH, CONNECTICUT

Ballet, as I've said, is my love when it comes to dance, and this enthusiasm helped me during my firm's creation of a stunning garden in Greenwich, Connecticut. Eric Groft, one of my partners at the firm, was the principal designer on this project, consulting with Wolfgang Oehme and myself.

This was an inspiring but also challenging opportunity. The house, a handsome nineteenth-century farmhouse, sits on a substantial tract of 25 acres. Most of that is wooded, but there is a cleared area of approximately 5 acres around the house, which was to be the object of our attentions. The clients had raised a family in the house, but by the time of our arrival on the scene, the children had moved out and the parents could indulge their own tastes. They wanted flowers, an English cottage look, and no lawn, aside from a small putting green where the master of the house could practice his golf and the grandchildren could play during visits.

So far, so good. But in classic farm fashion, the house had been set close to the road (what working farmer in the era of horse and wagon wanted a long driveway?), and the area behind the house dropped down a steep slope.

Circulation—how to get visitors and extended family members, as well as deliveries and tradespeople, in and out of the house while still preserving a sense of serenity and privacy—was going to be a challenge. We wanted a dance, not a series of collisions. At the same time, we had to turn the area behind the house into something other than an incipient land- ——— slide.

We solved the problem of access into and out of the house by moving the principal entrance so that instead of opening directly onto the fore-court, it was approached through an adjoining entry court and garden,

THE LILY POOL IN A
CONNECTICUT PERENNIAL
GARDEN AT THE HEIGHT
OF SUMMER.

THE LILY POOL WITH
RESIDENCE IN THE
DISTANCE AND STAIRWAY
DOWN FROM THE
FORECOURT.

PATH ACROSS THE REAR
OF THE HOUSE WITH THE
PORCH ON THE LEFT.

screened from the road by a high fence. A service entrance from the fore-court itself ensured convenient and separated access for deliveries. Then we terraced the site with a series of retaining walls of a granite suitably rugged for this New England location. The resulting asymmetric terraces allowed for a variety of experiences: a linear terrace garden that wrapped around the back of the house with prospects to the east, south, and north so that visitors could find sun or shade at any time of day, and a secluded court, centering on a lily pool, that encouraged lingering, providing pleasant pauses on the way up and down the flights of steps that led from one to the other. The flights of steps were offset or turned ninety degrees with respect to each other so that at no one point was the whole of the garden open to view, and each climb or descent remained modest and undaunting.

From below, down the hillside behind the house, the terraces seemed to set the house on a stage. The retaining walls, by extending the top of the hill, had steepened the grade of the hillside, turning it into something like a backdrop for the garden's lower level. Here we planted interwoven bursts of color. To suit our clients' taste for the cottage garden look, we used fewer grasses and even more perennials than we usually do in our designs. This exuberant dance of the flowers changes with the seasons, from daffodils and other bulbs in spring to landscape roses and tea viburnum, the snowballs of *Hydrangea arborescens* 'Annabelle' and the lavender mist of Russian sage (*Perovskia atriplicifolia*) in high summer, then lilac-flowered butterfly bush (*Buddleia davidii*) and the chrome yellow explosions of *Patrinia scabiosifolia* into fall. Paths swing down the hill from each side to intersect in the middle of the lower meadow, reinforcing the strongly rhythmic character of the new landscape.

The character of the paths was a particular concern in this highly choreographed garden. We interplanted the flagstones of the upper terrace with creeping herbs that release fragrances when stepped on. The steps running downward have treads of formal cut bluestone near the house but switch to rougher fieldstone as you descend into the meadow below, to signal the entry into a more informal setting. In the meadow, the surfacing of the paths changes again as you come into the less architectural, more natural area, from stone to a mulch. This is a garden you can read with your feet.

CONVERSATIONS WITH YO-YO MA AND JULIE MOIR MESSERVY

I can think of no more apt illustration of the interplay of different arts than the work of Yo-Yo Ma. He is famous, of course, for the virtuosity of his performances with the cello; he is also renowned for the versatility of his musical interests, which have ranged from Baroque chamber music to movie scores, traditional Chinese melodies, bluegrass, and tango. What is less well known, however, is his interest in gardens. He has commissioned gardens for both his houses from Julie Moir Messervy, a celebrated and imaginative Vermont-based landscape designer who is herself musically gifted (I remember sharing a speaking engagement with her and later coming down to the lobby of the hotel, impressed by the playing of a pianist there—then I saw it was Julie, relaxing at the keyboard). Yo-Yo Ma also collaborated with Julie on one of her most innovative projects, a "Music Garden" in Toronto.

Ma was making a series of six videos for public television, each of which was an exploration in partnership with a different artist of one of Bach's suites for unaccompanied cello. His collaboration with Julie centered on Suite #1. The city of Toronto made available three acres of reclaimed land along its riverfront, Ma played, and Julie translated his interpretation of the music into a garden with six distinct areas, each one corresponding to one of the suite's six movements.

Perhaps "translated" is not the right word (though I can think of no better one), because Julie's garden was not intended as a literal transcription of the music. Maybe she could have achieved that, for five of the six movements are based on different types of dances. Movement 2, for instance, is an *Allemande*, meaning that Bach adapted the movement's meter and tempo from a traditional German dance. Movement 5 is a *Menuett*, inspired by a French dance more familiar to us as the minuet. Julie could have tried to reiterate the rhythms and tempos in the same sequence, but she chose instead to treat both the garden and the music in a more abstract way—appropriately, in my opinion, since music is inherently an abstract art, as are the most exciting gardens.

Like the music that inspired it, Julie's composition uses flows—sometimes measured, elsewhere almost headlong—of visual notes framed in a crisp, clearly defined structure of paths and other architectural elements. Paths here do not meander aimlessly; they whirl and march and plunge. Julie used, for the most part, concrete poured in place—a pavement many disparage as characterless, but its plasticity enabled her to create clean-edged flows, as in the *Courante*, where the path spirals into a wildflower meadow, climbing toward a central maypole. It's part of the genius of this garden that it incorporates features such as the maypole, or the circular stage enclosed with an airy iron pavilion in the *Menuett*, that induce the visitor to join their own performance with that of the garden. The city government, incidentally, has reinforced this concept by hosting dance and musical performances on the stage, and readings in the *Sarabande*'s conifer grove that Julie envisioned as a poet's corner.

I also admire Julie's judicious use of regional details. She avoided a dogmatic insistence on native plants only, but did mix many indigenous

trees and perennials into her plantings and framed the undulating river-scape of the *Prelude* with powerful, locally sourced granite boulders.

I was fortunate to be able to interview both Yo-Yo Ma and Julie about the process of creating this garden, about the ways in which they let the music express itself in this landscape. I caught up with Julie Moir Messervy

in Cambridge, Massachusetts (where she has long maintained an office and studio), and later with Yo-Yo Ma (by telephone) before a performance in Houston, Texas. Given the nature of the subject, I've decided to let them express themselves in counterpoint.

THE *COURANTE* MOVE-MENT OF THE TORONTO MUSIC GARDEN.

About the inspiration
for the project:

YO-YO: One of the things I think Bach succeeded in doing almost more than anybody else is to suggest infinite variety. That was the key—the idea that anything that nature does is susceptible of infinite variety.

JULIE: I'd start with feeling, because for me . . . form follows feeling, it doesn't follow function. I don't sit down and do a program [an outline of the desired functions and uses] for a garden first [like most designers do] . . . I try to connect with my client on a feeling basis. And music is all about pure feeling. It's about flow and feeling. [And] that's what a garden is about—flow in the sense of paths, and feeling in the sense you're linking aspects of a place . . . form, color, shade, sun. It all suggests feelings and emotive qualities.

About the process of translating
music into landscape:

YO-YO: So what is a piece of music? What is a garden? It all requires nurturing, and the right context, and the right [execution] for something to grow . . . a piece of music is not series of notes you put down on a piece of paper. It's the coding of something . . . and in Bach's case, I think, the idea of infinite variety.

JULIE: What were the feelings I felt as I heard the music? And how did that translate? Obviously, happy vibrancy is bright colors. That's pretty obvious, right? . . . How did the feeling affect what the form might look like? What's an exuberant form, versus an inward, contemplative form? . . . And [what] was the imagery that came to my mind as I heard the music? I heard the *Courante* [movement 3] and saw in my mind's eye children in bright outfits dancing up this hillside. Well, what that meant when I actually translated it [into a section of the garden] was a spiraling path up to the top of the hill with a maypole at the top.

YO-YO: Well, how do you code that [the idea of infinite variety]? You could do it mathematically, you could do it in permutations, but [he coded it] in such a way that his music is both incredibly objective but also intensely personal. . . . So what do we have? What is our connection with nature? In some ways a lot and in some ways nothing. In other ways it's our perception of beauty and nature that is involved in the development, design, and planting of a garden.

About listening to, and seeing,

the vision in the music:

YO-YO: If you think of a piece of music as if you find a piece of DNA in [it], how does that DNA work in a very creative mind that is devoted to thinking in large part of the creation of gardens?

JULIE: Suite #1 had within it, embodied in it, some kind of DNA that was about landscape: flow, movement through space, verticality and horizontality. . . . I play the *Prelude* for people all the time. And when they hear it, I don't show them my design yet. "What do you hear?" They all hear riverscape. They all hear in and out, in and out, up and down, up and down. . . . The *Courante*, when I play that, the third movement, everybody hears birds, bees, butterflies. . . . They hear color, they hear bright, vibrant color. They hear big perennials. I saw children dancing. You just see things.

About how art expresses itself

through the landscape:

YO-YO: I learned from anthropology classes that agriculture came into our lives somewhere around ten thousand years ago. And so . . . a garden is probably one of our first art forms.

JULIE: I think it's a great litmus test for gardens: Does it flow? There is not a straight line—well, there are actually two straight lines—in that whole garden. They [the straight lines] are at the beginning of the *Prelude*. What I wanted to do was suggest meters, strict metric form. You know, signatures of the music and the meters as you move through a very flowy space, so that it gives you a sense of the fact that [the garden] marches through, but it flows. So I used very straight larches with black trunks—natives, I used a lot of natives in the garden. I planted them eighteen foot on center in the *Prelude* riverscape. That helped to start you off, but then after that, it's just all curve, all curve. You can see in the plan: C clefs, G clefs, F clefs. But I didn't mean them to be there. They just came out of the way [the paths and plantings] needed to flow.

About structure versus detail:

JULIE: It [the garden] is really, in the end, six separate movements—just as the structure of the music—that flow together as one large form. The way I show the difference is usually by [a change in] plant material, and often a key threshold of some sort that links the two. I really needed a gateway between the *Menuett* pavilion, which is a performance space, and the *Gigue* [jig] area that is much more energetic. So I used two weeping birch trees. You know, one curtsies and the other bows. Literally—I mean, we chose them for that.

About involving the public in the art:

YO-YO: What I love about it is that for many people . . . it's all four seasons. . . . People go there, people have weddings there, they have concerts there. The harbor is right next to it, the residential apartments, there are people that really take care of the garden. There's an elementary school nearby, [the students] go to it.

JULIE: What I did with the music garden was I played the music for everyone I possibly could, so that they would join me in making this thing a work of art. I played it for the construction workers. . . . And they'd say,

"Julie, should we bring this rock over to the *Allemande?*" It was beautiful. They all came to the opening because they all felt they had contributed to this big piece of music in the garden. The guy who did the wrought-iron structure. The woman who did the maypole. Everyone got involved.

Finally, though, it was one of Yo-Yo Ma's remarks that impressed me most deeply. It expressed not only the depth of his artistry, but also clarified for me something I have felt about gardening but have never managed to articulate so clearly:

"One of the things I've been thinking about a lot lately and talking to younger people about," he said to me, "as well as telling myself, is that part of doing any art form is to transcend technique. . . . One of the core values I was taught when I was younger . . . is that you're working for something bigger than yourself. So it's not how *I* do this. Rather, you're going toward something which is the codification of a piece of music or art form or whatever. You're working with your disciplined imagination. And you're working with other people's imaginations. . . . We're working toward a common imagination that is bigger than what we are."

What we can translate into our art from other forms—music and dance, or painting, whatever you like—is not just technique. There's also an understanding about purpose. By listening and looking at the accomplishments of masters like Yo-Yo Ma, or Julie Moir Messervy, we see an example of where, if we strive, our own art can take us.

5

TEXTURE

The Fabric of the Garden

I search for the realness, the real feeling of a subject, all the texture around it. . . . I always want to see the third dimension of something. . . . I want to come alive with the object.

—ANDREW WYETH

The web, then, or the pattern, a web at once sensuous and logical, an elegant and pregnant texture: that is style.

—ROBERT LOUIS STEVENSON

VIEW OVER THE POND AT FERRY COVE, MY WEEKEND RETREAT, WITH THE GUEST HOUSE ON THE LEFT AND THE MAIN HOUSE ON THE RIGHT.

When I plan a garden, I do not think in terms of borders and beds, or even of paths and meadows. These and other elements may all play roles in the design (though probably not beds and borders—such nice, neat, confined gestures are a bit too timid). But a garden designed piecemeal, one bit at a time, is bound to be a failure. Instead, I visualize a garden as a tapestry. The beauty or interest derives from how you weave all the different elements together into a whole. In that sense, I tend to imagine gardens as textures.

Texture is, in my opinion, the most underused resource in the garden design toolbox. We pay lip service to it. We speak admiringly of the texture of individual plants, their tactile surfaces, the impression made by the size and character of their foliage or bark. Those things are certainly worthy of notice and can be quite useful to the garden maker. But texture is far more than this. If you explore the original meaning of the word, you'll find that "texture" derives from words meaning "to weave" and that initially it was used to describe any woven object (or "web"). That's how I like to think of texture even now: as the fundamental tapestry, the substance of the garden as a whole.

Even when you use texture in the more limited contemporary sense of the word, however, as encompassing no more than the surfaces of plants and objects in your garden, this remains an unusually potent design tool. It is the only effect I can think of that we perceive with two senses. We learn textures with our sense of touch: we describe something as "smooth as silk" because at some point we felt how easily a bit of silk slips through our fingers. Over time, though, we learn to recognize textures visually. Just seeing the fuzzy, silvered surface of *Stachys byzantina*, the plant we commonly call "lamb's ear," stimulates our recollection of similar surfaces and is enough to tell us just how the touch of those leaves against our cheek will feel.

I suspect that it is texture's link to memory that makes this quality so evocative. You see the spiky texture of a holly's foliage and you remember the discomfort of pruning that prickly shrub last spring. You see a thistle, or even a thistlelike *Eryngium* or "sea holly" (a gorgeous, striking plant), and somewhere in your mind you hark back to what you felt when you stumbled into a patch of thistles as a child. In this way, texture possesses the power not only to gratify or repel touch and vision, but also to provoke emotional responses. That's why, I suspect, we have borrowed so many textural terms to describe other things. If we say a cheap wine tastes *rough* while a better one is *smooth,* the listener knows what our judgment is, though in fact the flavor has nothing to do with texture. Likewise, we may characterize someone's manners as coarse or fine, a devious person as slippery, and a strong face as rugged good looks. If we use the evocative potential of texture skillfully in our garden design, we can influence how the landscape makes a person feel.

MANAGING TEXTURES WITHIN THE GARDEN

There are many potential sources of texture for the garden.

Stones, for example, can serve to introduce rugged textures or, in the case of rounded river rocks, a smooth and finished one. Built elements, such as decks, paths, and terraces, all contribute textures, and the same material may function very differently depending on how we use and finish it—a path of cut stone pavers, for example, has a very different texture than one of rough fieldstone. Different mulches have different textures (compare the fine texture of pine needles, a southern favorite, with the rougher surface of shredded bark), and even exposed soils can be a source of texture. All of these textures can and should be used in a calculated fashion by the designer. By far the greatest variety of textures, however, and the ones that ordinarily predominate in a garden, are those of plant foliages. Flowers, too, offer textures—compare the in-your-face disk of a sunflower with the lavender mist that hovers over a Russian sage in bloom—but flowers pass in and out of season. For most of any growing season, the texture that a plant delivers, day after day, is that of its foliage, and in the case of trees and shrubs, their twigs and branches.

SMOOTH RIVER STONES
USED AS MULCH BY
ROBERTO BURLE MARX.

The texture that predominates in most American landscapes, to the near exclusion of everything else, is the close-clipped nap of lawn. Well-maintained turf grasses offer a texture that's invitingly lush and soft, but it's also a bland one. Making that the mainstay of your garden is like selecting cream of wheat as the staple of your diet. I include some areas of lawn in my designs for functional reasons, as play areas for children or as a surface for outdoor entertainment spaces. But quite apart from the environmental costs of lawns—the unsustainable investments of fertilizers, pesticides, and water they require and the air and noise pollution caused by the constant mowing—I dislike lawn's status as the default landscape surface because it represents missed opportunities. Unless there is a genuine need for turf (of the sort I cited above), a lawn reflects a missed opportunity for self-expression and for a more thoughtful, rewarding relationship to the natural riches all around us.

WHAT DETERMINES THE TEXTURAL
EFFECT OF A FOLIAGE

When considered in this more limited sense, a plant's texture fundamentally derives from the physical form of the foliage. Small or fine leaves, like those of rosemarys and lavenders, or of creeping thymes, all give an impression of fine textures, as does one of my favorite ornamental grasses—*Hakonechloa macra*, Japanese forest grass. Needled evergreens also contribute fine textures, as do such deciduous shrubs as the purple osier willow (*Salix purpurea*) or the various cotoneasters. A more delicate, almost filigreed, texture is that of the finely cut leaves of Japanese maples. Bolder textures are typical of the big-leaved hostas; a Midwestern coneflower I particularly like, *Rudbeckia fulgida*, which has good-sized blue-green leaves; or (at the extreme end of bold) the ornamental rhubarbs (*Gunnera* spp.), whose leaves can measure six feet across.

As I mentioned at the beginning of this chapter, however, our perception of textures is largely visual, and so the way in which a foliage reflects light also plays a role in determining a plant's apparent texture. A glossy, reflective surface enhances the effect of a foliage's texture. The finely cut foliage of "Silver King" artemisia looks all the more delicate because the silver leaves are covered with glistening hairs, while the waxy sheen of the heart-shaped leaves of European ginger (*Asarum europaeum*) makes this species one of the most visible and boldest groundcovers for shady areas. Dull-surfaced foliages tend to recede into the background visually, making their textures less pronounced. Brightly colored or variegated foliages are more visible, and thus their textures are more conspicuous. Surface textures also influence our perception of other aspects of a plant's foliage. The glossy, satiny texture of the heuchera's leaves, for instance, is what gives a peculiar richness to the plum color of this foliage; the translucence of rose petals is what gives them their special delicacy and depth of tint.

WAYS OF USING INDIVIDUAL TEXTURES

In many respects, textures serve a landscape in ways parallel to those of color and form. That is, by combining related textures you can create harmonies, and by juxtaposing strongly contrasting textures you can inject drama. Repeating a strongly distinctive texture—typically, an eye-catching, bold one—at calculated intervals creates a rhythm within the landscape.

Contrasting textures can also be used to emphasize their neighbors. Think of how the boulders and ledges of a rock garden accentuate the delicacy of the alpine flowers—creeping phloxes or miniature bulbs, for example—planted amid them. This is one of the really effective uses of lawn: a surrounding of turf does accentuate the ruggedness of a mature tree or trees, a gnarled live oak, say, or a massive old cedar of Lebanon—though a surround of meadow would accomplish the same end in a much more interesting and environmentally desirable fashion.

I like to play off the setting in my use of textures. Around a small, confined courtyard or terrace, I prefer to use bold-textured, big-leaved plants; I've found that the obvious (and often recommended) response of sticking to less assertive, fine-textured plants in such a setting creates an insipid prettiness. Sometimes, however, the opposite extreme can be effective—I think of the small urban gardens in Japan where an architecturally enclosed space may be planted with nothing more than a few well-chosen rocks, perhaps some moss, and a single clump of slender-stemmed bamboo. In situations such as those, the heaviness of the setting emphasizes the fineness and flexibility of the bamboo, accentuating its inherent grace.

We have always favored bold-textured plants at my firm: *Yucca filamentosa*, sacred lotus (*Nelumbo nucifera*), *Ligularia dentata*, and (before we discovered that it can be invasive) the magnificent Japanese butterbur, *Petasites japonicus* var. *giganteus*, whose veined, round leaves can expand to a diameter of four feet. We use these species to focus our plantings and serve as a counterpoise to the finer textures of our meadowlike tapestries of grasses and perennials.

Incidentally, I would also advise that the finer textures you incorporate into your designs you plant in generous swaths or clusters. Otherwise they, too, will subside into the background, for all practical purposes simply disappearing from the scene.

DESIGN INSIGHTS
FROM PIET OUDOLF

For more than twenty years, Dutchman Piet Oudolf has been one of the most innovative and sought-after garden designers in Europe. Over the last decade, he has become a force in American gardens as well, creating a number of definitive public landscapes including the Garden of Remembrance in Manhattan's Battery Park and the planting design for New York's High Line Park (a 1.5-mile-long landscape on top of an abandoned elevated railroad) that opened to general acclamation in 2009, as well as the Lurie Garden in Chicago's Millennium Park.

Oudolf is also famous for his unconventional understanding of garden design. Unlike the great bulk of gardeners who look to a flower's color first, Oudolf begins by looking at its form—globular or saucer-shaped, spiky or plumelike—and how the individual blossoms on a plant relate to each other and the plant as a whole. The "skeletons" of the plants, he explains, are as important to him as the flowers. Oudolf is notorious for insisting that clients not cut back and tidy up the gardens in fall as is the American habit: an essential element of his designs is the tapestry of russets and browns, or seedheads and withered stems, the garden presents in winter.

My partner Sheila Brady visited Piet during a trip to the Netherlands, to explore with him his design style.

The process:
I start with a theme, with a concept. I have a rough idea and then the rough idea means that you have an overall idea about the height, more or less, the expression of the low [part of the garden]. That's how you start. Then you think of course within the theme [playing with different means of expression].

I think more or less in calm or vibrant, or just movement, strong or soft. . . . At first I think of what [I need to achieve with the design, the practical uses of the space] and the overall feeling of the garden.

THE WALLED GARDEN AT BURY COURT GARDENS, BENTLEY, SURREY, UNITED KINGDOM, DESIGNED BY PIET OUDOLF.

Oudolf explains that although he is famous for his plantsmanship—he operates a very successful nursery that has introduced many new plants onto the market—his plant combinations are not based on calculation but instead on intuition, improvisation, and on-the-spot inspiration: "When I look at a garden, I see more music and rhythm but also I envision it in the abstract expressionist style of De Kooning. I am not a musician, but I can feel what happens when I am designing. I am a visual person. My life is all about images. I create images that live." (The Dutch-born De Kooning is famous for, among other things, the development of action painting, an intuitive style in which paint is dribbled, smeared, or splashed onto the canvas so that the work becomes becomes the record of the

process of creation, almost like a musical score. The way in which De Kooning applied paint—sometimes thickly with a palette knife, sometimes in drips or dabs or slaps of the brush—gave his paintings strongly textural surfaces.)

"Color should not be necessary," Oudolf continued. "Color is expression, but it does not make the garden. . . . It is essential that everything you do should be [visualized] in black and white." In fact, Oudolf uses only

black and white in working out his designs until late in the process, when, to help establish what the color patterns will be, he reaches for colored pencils.

"If the structure is right, the garden works. It doesn't matter what colors you use," Oudolf stresses.

CREATING THE ILLUSION OF
DEPTH WITH TEXTURES

I've already described how the owner of a small plot can give it an impression of greater depth by manipulating the color (see page 83) or by forcing the perspective (see page 97). You can achieve a similar effect through the use of plant textures. This relies on the fact that the apparent size of objects decreases with distance from the viewer. More simply put, distant objects look small, whereas ones nearby tend to look larger. Reversing this natural progression by planting finer-textured plants in the background of your garden and coarser-textured ones in the foreground creates the impression that the background of the garden is more distant than it actually is.

Juxtaposing textures can also draw a viewer's eyes to a particular plant or object and shape their impression of it. A gnarled dwarf evergreen looks even more rugged and ancient when silhouetted against a background of fine-textured perennials, and miniature narcissi look even more dainty when backed by large-leaved rhododendrons. And don't forget that the built elements in a garden have textures, too, and can contribute to such juxtapositions. A tendril of *Clematis texensis* with its nodding, rose-colored blossoms will look exquisitely fine when clambering over a rough stone wall, just as an antique Japanese stone lantern looks even more stalwart and enduring when displayed in front of fine-needled pines.

WEAVING AND REWEAVING AT FERRY COVE

In some respects it's the dream commission—when you design a garden for yourself, you get a client who agrees with you on every point. At the same time, though, you have to actually live with the results. That's why, when I undertook to build myself a weekend house, "Ferry Cove," on the Eastern Shore of the Chesapeake Bay, I proceeded very deliberately.

As the son of a builder, and as someone who studied architecture, I've always felt that someday I ought to build a house of my own. This seemed the perfect opportunity. In 1996 I'd found a 25-acre soybean field at the edge of the Chesapeake Bay in Maryland's Eastern Shore. I've mentioned in a previous chapter (see page 70) sculptor and painter Anne Truitt's attachment to this region and how it figured in her work. I, too, love the Eastern Shore. I'm from Dutch stock and spent three and a half years in the Netherlands as a young man. I still consider it my second home, and of all the places I've been in the United States, it's the Eastern Shore that reminds me most of the Netherlands. The spreading vistas and subtle topography, the intersection of the plane of the water with the plane of the land, the vast sky—the two areas share all these defining characteristics.

I bought the land in partnership with two friends. I didn't want to keep all of the acreage, but I also wanted to make sure that my neighbors wouldn't create some sort of architectural status symbol and spoil the rural beauty of the place. Then I took my time getting to know the three acres along the shore that I kept for myself. Almost every weekend for a year after buying the land, I'd drive out from Washington to stay at an Eastern Shore inn so that I could walk the land, spend time on it just absorbing. I spent another full year working out the planting design while the house (designed by Suman Sorg, a brilliant architect who has partnered with me on projects all over the world) went up. I wanted to savor this project in a leisurely way, and I wanted to be sure I was creating something worthy of this special site.

With the Bay, the largest estuary in the United States, at its foot, I

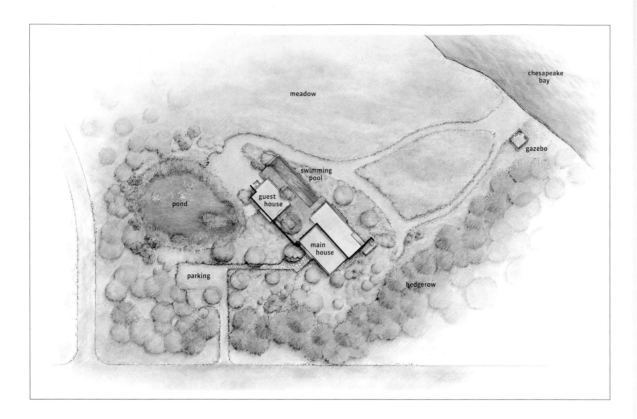

Labels within image: chesapeake bay, meadow, gazebo, swimming pool, guest house, pond, main house, parking, hedgerow

FERRY COVE ON
MARYLAND'S EASTERN
SHORE.

VIEW OVER THE MEADOW
TOWARD THE HOUSE AT
FERRY COVE.

knew the garden would have to be a strong one if it wasn't to look insignificant. What I didn't want was the sort of "pretty" garden that is so easily assembled from mass-marketed perennials. I wanted, I explained to one friend, Noel Kingsbury, an *ugly* garden, one full of the sort of big, coarse, assertive plants that could hold their own with such a view and complement the shoreline's feeling of untamed nature. Noel, who's an internationally recognized garden designer in his own right and has collaborated with Piet Oudolf on two books, laughed, but I know from looking at his work that he understood.

I also wanted to preserve intact the ecology of the site. For this reason, I decided to use a plant list consisting almost entirely of species native to the area, and to design the garden as a meadow, the sort of grassland that quite likely existed on the site long ago, before it was first plowed up for agriculture. For help with this aspect of the design, I turned

BRONZE SNAKE SWIMMING
POOL HANDRAIL BY
SCULPTOR RAY KASKEY,
WITH MEADOW AND
CHESAPEAKE BAY BEYOND.

to Darrel Morrison, a landscape architect, and at that time a professor at the University of Georgia, who has specialized in ecological design. He suggested that I watch to see what naturally emerged on the site now that it was no longer being farmed. The first year, a blanket of horsetails (*Equisetum arvense*) sprang up. This plant is as colorful as its name, a spore-bearing plant that is a survivor from the age of the dinosaurs. As I looked out admiringly over the bright green plumed expanse, I wondered how long that plant had been lying dormant in the soil. The next year, grasses began to pop up, mostly little bluestem (*Schizachyrium scoparium*) and switchgrass (*Panicum virgatum*). These last two species, stalwart prairie natives, I made keynotes of my planting.

To screen the inland perimeter of the garden, I planted a variety of native trees, all species with strong foliages: glossy-leaved American holly (*Ilex opaca*); sweetgums (*Liquidambar styraciflua*), whose star-shaped leaves turn a brilliant red, purple, or orange in fall; catalpas (*Catalpa*

DRIFTWOOD GAZEBO BY BEN FORGEY WITH LOWES WHARF ON THE FAR LEFT.

VIEW OVER THE MEADOW
IN AUTUMN TOWARD THE
CHESAPEAKE BAY. THE
GAZEBO IS ON THE RIGHT.

bignonioides), whose heart-shaped leaves can measure eight inches across and that bear large bunches of orchidlike white, purple, and yellow flowers in early summer; and southern magnolias (*Magnolia grandiflora*), whose long, evergreen leaves make an elegant background for the fragrant white saucer-shaped flowers the tree bears from spring into summer. Not ugly, you say? Perhaps not; but certainly assertive.

The side of the yard facing the road (to the southwest of the house) I domesticated just slightly, excavating a pond, which I planted with water lilies (*Nymphaea* sp.), hardy cannas (*Thalia dealbata*), wild rice (*Zizania latifolia*), and bulrush (*Scirpus lacustris*). Around this I wove a dense web of perennials: asters, select clones of native grasses (such as switchgrass 'Cloud Nine'), and grassland perennials such as achilleas, *Rudbeckia maxima*, tradescantias, bigleaf mountain mint (*Pycnanthemum muticum*), sunflowers, false indigo, and the magnificently coarse cup (*Silphium perfo-*

THE FRONT WALK AT
FERRY COVE, WITH
PARKING IN THE
DISTANCE AND A GRACE
KNOWLTON BALL.

liatum), which can reach a height of ten feet, bearing clusters of yellow daisylike blossoms atop stout, hairy stems embraced by cuplike pockets of big sandpapery leaves.

At Ferry Cove, I planted not in clusters of each kind in traditional gardenesque style, but instead thoroughly intermingled the different plants as you would find them in a meadow. I reinforced the perennials and grasses with a scattering of shrubs: viburnums and deutzias, but also less well known stalwarts such as groundseltree *(Baccharis halimifolia),* a semi-evergreen native of the coastal areas in the eastern United States, and the rosemary willow *(Salix elaeagnos),* another local native. The path from the parking area I surfaced with crushed oyster shells, a traditional paving material in this region and one very much in harmony with the seaside location.

The house, which faces the bay, is set fully 250 feet back from the shore. I continued the interwoven planting of perennials and shrubs around this side in a band fifty feet deep. Beyond this is a strip of mowed grass (invisible from the house and deck), and beyond that, native meadow extending down to the beach. I irrigated during the first year after planting the landscape, but have not done so since, and I do not fertilize. I mow the meadows periodically, and I weed when some interloper threatens to take over—though when I like the look of the volunteer, I leave it in place. I like to think of my garden as a living filter that catches any precipitation and runoff, straining it through the plant roots and cleansing it biologically before releasing it into the bay. In an era when nearby communities are finding it necessary to ban lawn fertilizers to reduce the pollution load in the bay, I cannot help thinking how helpful it would be if other gardeners began redeveloping their plots along similar lines.

As always, the creation of this garden has involved a lot of learning along the way and some unanticipated pleasures. In particular, I had never realized what a wonderful small tree the common hackberry (*Celtis occidentalis*) is. Not a pretty one: the bark is corky and covered with what look like warts, and the twigs zigzag irregularly. The tree definitely has a mind of its own, sending off new growth in all sorts of unexpected directions. I'm convinced it has a sense of humor; at any rate, it makes me laugh. It's fast-growing, too, so that after a dozen years the one I planted next to the deck already provides all the shade I need. I've been able to retire the umbrellas I used to set up for that purpose, so I no longer need to retrieve them after every windstorm.

Over time, the garden is adjusting my design to better suit the site. The plants sow themselves into hospitable niches, finding spots they like better than the ones I gave them. And though I kept the sightline to the shore empty to maximize the view, I've found I like the wild junipers (*Juniperus virginiana*) that are springing up along the beach to divide the visual expanse into more limited, randomly framed vistas. Let the garden reweave itself.

A CONVERSATION WITH JACK LENOR LARSEN

"Think of yourself as a spider!"

—JACK LENOR LARSEN

I like to think of myself as a tapestry maker; Jack Lenor Larsen actually is one. Although, to be accurate, he is many other things as well. From the moment he opened his first textile studio in New York, his extraordinary work attracted the attention of equally extraordinary people. Within months, Alexander Calder, Leonard Bernstein, and I. M. Pei were wearing one-of-a-kind ties he had handwoven with his fibers and to his specifications, and the Duke of Windsor was wearing a suit cut from Larsen cloth. He was much more than a society phenomenon, however. Jack Lenor Larsen almost single-handedly moved weaving and textile design from the status of folk or industrial craft to one of fine art. The way in which he wove together disparate materials—straw, bamboo, raffia, wire, rope, and even rags as well as the traditional silks, cottons, wools, and linens—in combination with his inspired mastery of color and the architecture of textiles, overturned people's understanding of the field. Larsen textiles helped contribute pattern and texture to Frank Lloyd Wright's Taliesin house in Wisconsin, and he also helped Edgar Kaufman, Jr. find weavings

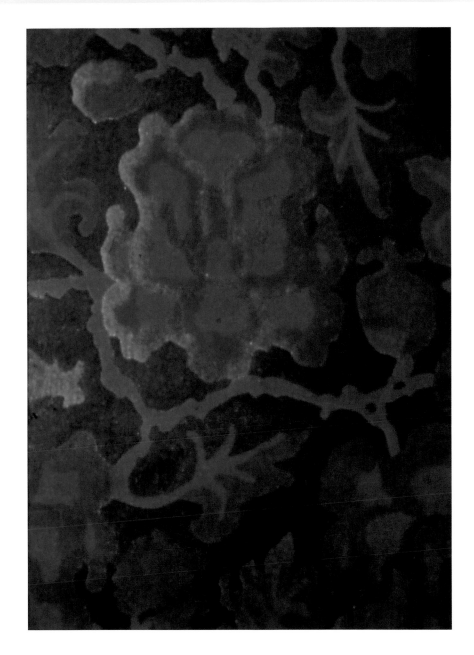

to enrich the family's retreat in southwest Pennsylvania, Fallingwater. In a more populist vein, he has, through highly successful collections of textiles—carpeting, towels, sheets, and drapes—designed for retailers such as Bloomingdale's and Macy's, had a notable impact on middle-class America's taste.

Long before Larsen first put his hands to a loom, however, he was already an enthusiastic and unconventional gardener. He began planting, he told me, "when I was two. I was in Seattle, and I was given some radish seeds and shown how to plant them and cover them with cheesecloth to prevent flies from getting in and so forth. I had a crop in six weeks. And with that success, I was off and running."

The next year he collected maple seedlings to start planting a more permanent garden. When his family went for Sunday rides, if they passed a promising area, he would say, "Let me out here with my shovel." He would prospect for wildflowers, ferns, and mosses, bringing home the best for his ever-expanding plantings.

A peripatetic existence during his years as a student and then as a young textile designer interfered with Larsen's ability to practice as a gardener. But the purchase of twelve and then four more acres in the town of East Hampton at the end of Long Island presented him with an opportunity to close a circle and integrate his old love for the landscape with the experience and skills he had acquired as a designer. Larsen built a 13,000-square-foot structure styled after a seventh-century Shinto shrine he had come to love during trips to Japan. The building, "LongHouse," whose interior space can be reconfigured with the use of sliding screens covered with his own textiles, has served not only as a weekend home but also as a museum and a teaching and performance space. The surrounding land he turned into a sculpture garden complete with amphitheater and dramatic, meticulously interwoven plantings.

It's more than just a figure of speech to describe Larsen's garden, "LongHouse Reserve," in terms of weaving—he is explicit about the connection between the two crafts. He has written about how as a beginning weaver he tried to express in fibers the furrowed rows of planted fields. Later, as a student at the University of Southern California, he wove into his textiles leaves, pods, and cones that he collected during bicycle rides.

When he was called upon to create a carpet for the lobby of the Joyce Theater, a leading dance venue in New York, Larsen found inspiration in a Japanese red maple in his garden. Looking up through the canopy of foliage, he realized that it was both red and green but that the two hues were of exactly the same intensity—"particularly the same value infused into each other, even though they were complements [i.e., the strongest of contrasts]. Could I do that with fabric? It worked very well. . . . In that carpet, I used reds against greens and several greens and several reds." He dubbed that carpet design "Fantasy." Larsen has become known for his experiments with complementary hues in the same values, counterpoises of pale lavender and gold, for example, which he says he also observed in the garden.

The inspiration has gone both ways, Larsen adds. "Early on, I heard a young philosopher expound . . . that we only see in nature what we learn in art. And I think that's very true, that maybe the purpose of art is to help us see relationships, associations with things in nature, in everyday life. I find that's often true, that I understand in nature what I have first learned in art, one way or another."

Larsen views nature with the eye of an artist who has spent decades analyzing the interplay of colors and textures. He wrote in *A Weaver's Memoir*, his personal testament, that in walking among the eastern Long Island dunes, for instance, he enjoys "the nuance of highlight and shadow of gray foliage, or the shadow of wiry grass stalks bending with the wind to trace concentric circles on the sand." He played with these effects in the "dune garden" he created with sandy soil excavated from the cellar hole of his house. Silver-leaved santolinas and dusty millers, gray cypresses and rugosa roses were interwoven with dune grasses to make that tapestry.

He loves the interplay of color and texture displayed in the exfoliat-

ing bark of such trees as sycamores, Chinese birches (*Albo-sinensis*), and the native river birch (*Betula nigra*). However beautiful he may find any single such thread, though, Larsen never loses sight of the web as a whole. He tends, for example, to avoid juxtaposing strong color contrasts in the flower garden so as not to fix the viewer's attention on a single spot. He wants the focus to remain on the composition in its entirety.

"My new feeling," he told me, "is that flower color [is extraneous]—everyone seems focused on the flowers, which are going to bloom for two weeks, when making the decisions [about the planting and design]. . . . I've been to Japan forty times, usually in winter, and their gardens are as wonderful in winter as in summer. They don't pay much attention to flowers; they're like jewelry. . . . They don't plan around flower color. And less and less do I. . . . The sculpture of the trees, the forms and branching pattern, bark color, all of that is so much more satisfying. It makes winter a blessing. . . ."

One way in which Larsen has found gardening and weaving to be very different is that a garden is dynamic—it changes all the time. He's used to designing with the various elements as they are, not trying to visualize how they will be in a year or a decade. This makes scale particularly challenging for him—when looking at a young tree and deciding how it fits into the fabric, he has trouble coping with the fact that it will expand to many times its current size. The device he has developed is deliberately overplanting. The allée of ten-foot-tall cryptomerias with which he framed the entrance to the LongHouse property, for example, he set close for an immediate effect. Three years later, when the trees were twenty feet tall, he hired an arborist with a hydraulic tree spade to transplant every second tree, giving the remaining ones room to spread. This may seem extravagant, but in fact it provided Larsen with a quantity of twenty-foot trees (purchased at the much lower ten-foot price) to provide instant screening of the property's north boundary.

Jack Larsen has transferred ownership of the house and gardens, arguably his greatest tapestry, to a nonprofit to ensure its preservation and the continuation of its work of education. The LongHouse website describes those gardens as "an expansive case study of a considered lifestyle at the turn of the millennium. The objective is to simultaneously create landscapes as an art form and to demonstrate planting potentials in this climate—with broad selections of species and cultivars."

True enough; but I prefer Jack Larsen's more succinct summation. "Think of yourself as a spider," he urges his fellow gardeners. "Think of cocoons and hornets' nests, all those natural fabrics that are so beautiful and not just flat." Think of that, indeed, when you next take your spade from the toolshed.

6

LAYERING FOR MYSTERY AND ENTICEMENT

The job of the artist is always to
deepen the mystery.

—FRANCIS BACON

Nobody reads a mystery to get to the middle.
They read it to get to the end. If it's a letdown,
they won't buy any more. The first page sells that
book. The last page sells your next book.

—MICKEY SPILLANE

PERENNIAL GARDEN
WITH LILY POOL AT A
HOME IN VIRGINIA.

The promise—maybe unspoken, but still there—of most works about garden design is that the expert and author is going to take the mystery out of this process. That's a mistake. What I want to do in this chapter is the exact opposite: I want to put mystery back into the heart of garden design, where it needs to be. Mystery is an essential element of any really pleasurable garden. It's what lures you in through the

MARTHA SCHWARTZ,
FIELD WORK, 1997.
SPOLETO FESTIVAL,
CHARLESTON,
SOUTH CAROLINA.

gate, keeps you moving from spot to spot through the landscape, and fills you with excitement along the way. The sense of mystery is what turns a mere display of plants, paths, and ornaments into an adventure. Don't worry, though. I intend to do this in an unmysterious way, because creating mystery, ironically enough, turns out to be a straightforward process.

LAYERING

I can, if I close my eyes, still see the garden behind my childhood home in Grand Rapids, Michigan. A rectangle of lawn edged with rosebushes, flowers, and other plantings, it was meticulously kept, but not at all interesting. One glance and you had taken in all there was to see.

Until my mother hung out the wash. She'd pin the sheets, shirts, and other clothes to the lines that stretched across the yard, and all of a sudden you were peering around and through the laundry layers to assemble an impression from dozens of different glimpses and perspectives. A most obvious spot had been unintentionally endowed with mystery.

This vision came back to me when I saw photographs of a brilliant installation that landscape architect Martha Schwartz created for the Spoleto Festival in Charleston, South Carolina, in 1997. (Lisa Delplace, one of my current partners, worked with Martha at the time and was involved in creating the installation.) The site of the installation, which Martha dubbed *Field Work,* was an old plantation on the outskirts of the city. There Martha erected poles connected by wires running in parallel like giant laundry lines from the slave cabins out into an adjacent field. From the wires she hung thousands of white sheets (actually pieces of a semitransparent stage set material called "scrim"), and she whitewashed the grass paths in between. The effect was ghostly as the sheets flapped in the wind; with her simple apparatus, Martha exposed the many layers of the place and the maze of boundaries and barriers that had characterized it, using nothing more than the stylized contents of a slave woman's washbasket.

WHEN YOU'VE GOT IT, DON'T FLAUNT IT

What's my message? It's a natural instinct in most of us that when we've got something exceptional, we want to show it off. But if you give in to this impulse in your garden too uninhibitedly, making your prize view or botanical rarity immediately apparent as you first enter the landscape, you squander all potential for surprise and wonder. You make the rest of the landscape anticlimactic. Why should visitors bother to explore any farther?

At the beginning of this book, I compared gardens to sculpture, which is work in three dimensions. That comparison is useful, but it doesn't tell the whole story because a garden is constructed in four dimensions. As well as length, width, and height, there is also time. You must consider time when designing a garden in part because, as Jack Lenor Larsen observed (see page 159), the materials you work with in this craft are largely living ones, which change size and, commonly, shape and appearance with time's passage. If you don't consider this process of chronological evolution, you lay up all sorts of problems for yourself in your planting. How many times have you seen some house claustrophobically overshadowed by giant Norway spruces that had been set on either side of the front steps when they were cute little Christmas trees? On a recent trip to Portland, Oregon, I saw what must be the ultimate example of this. A few blocks from the entrance to the city's Japanese garden (a must-see if you are ever in that city) was a modest brick house whose concrete front walk had been half swallowed by the six-foot-thick trunks of the pair of redwoods that had been planted, clearly as saplings, a couple of feet to either side. You could hardly squeeze between the trees anymore, and indeed the whole front yard and the house itself looked utterly insignificant in comparison.

Designers must also consider this fourth dimension, time, when practicing their craft, because a well-planned garden is not one but a sequence of experiences. These experiences may take many forms: a spot where you are embraced by the scents of aromatic herbs, a seat that faces you toward a beautiful vista, a walk through a flowery meadow, the fountain whose trickling water music soothes you at the end of a busy day. I've already alluded in my discussion of dance and choreography to the importance of arranging these experiences in a calculated manner. One of the simplest and yet most effective tools for accomplishing this, as my mother demonstrated to me many decades ago, is layering.

A GRAVEL PATH MEANDERS TOWARD THE ARBOR IN A WALLED GARDEN MY FIRM DESIGNED FOR AN ESTATE ON LANGFORD CREEK ON MARYLAND'S EASTERN SHORE. RESIDENCE IN THE DISTANCE.

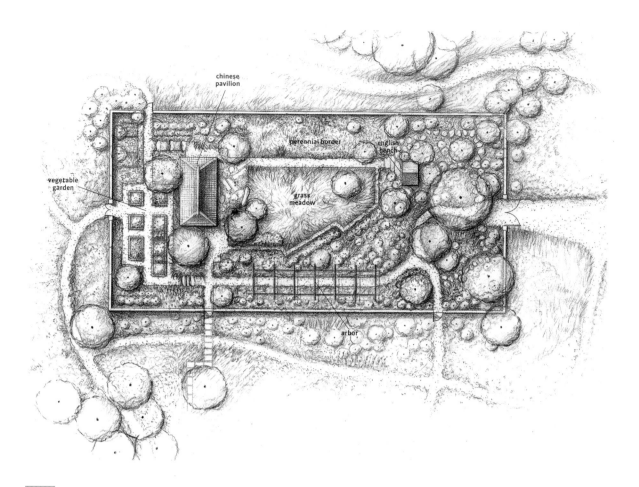

Labels within illustration:
chinese pavilion

perennial border

english bench

vegetable garden

grass meadow

arbor

PLAN OF THE ENGLISH-INSPIRED WALLED GARDEN.

WHAT'S INVOLVED

Remember the country retreat that my client described as "the garden of the seven veils" (page 24)? My partner Eric Groft's use of informal masses of tall perennials and grasses to create boundaries within a flat landscape and isolate (at least partially) areas designed for different activities is a prime example of the use of layering.

What you use to create the layers can be all sorts of things: shrubbery, trees, fences or walls of various heights, trellises. I've used copper panels for this purpose—stones—even sculpture. In the tiny backyard of my former house in Washington's Georgetown neighborhood, I used an evergreen sweetbay magnolia (*Magnolia virginiana*). This tree, which can grow to a height of sixty feet, was by most standards out of scale for the space, which measured just 55 feet by 17 feet. The garden was designed not for walking but rather for viewing, from double doors at the back of the kitchen. I placed the magnolia in the foreground so that you looked through its branches to view the rest of the garden, adding complexity to what would otherwise have been a too-obvious vista.

Don't think of layering in terms of barriers. Though some types of devices used for this purpose, such as walls and fences, commonly serve as layering, too, they don't function in this sense by physically blocking your passage. The metaphor for layering I like best is that of a theatrical scrim, a curtain made of the type of gauzy material Martha Schwartz used for her Spoleto installation. In the theater, a scrim is hung across the stage, commonly partway back. When lit from the front, the scrim is opaque. When backlit, however, the fabric becomes transparent wherever the light hits it, revealing part of what is hidden behind it. Scrims are commonly used to create a dreamlike atmosphere—as the main action of the play carries on in front of the scrim, figures or props appear and disappear, as spotlights are turned on and off, like memories or visions.

Unlike Martha Schwartz, I have never hung actual scrims in the landscape, but for layering I do prefer to use materials or objects, both living and man-made, that direct or deflect the view without banning it altogether. The goal is not to discourage garden visitors, but rather to mystify them and lure them on.

A PLOT FOR YOUR PLOT

Another useful model I have found for thinking about layering and its uses is a literary one. In this sense, gardeners can learn something from any accomplished mystery writer.

Reread the quote from Mickey Spillane at the opening of this chapter. My own taste doesn't run to stories about tough guys and blondes, but Spillane's sales (225 million books by the time of his death in 2006) proves he knew how to reach an audience.

Am I suggesting you need a corpse and smoking gun in the opening scene of your garden? No. But it helps to think of the garden as a series of connected scenes, much like the plot of a novel, all coordinating in a single, extended adventure. It also helps to remember, as Spillane says, that you have to seize the visitors' attention with their first glance, and keep them sufficiently intrigued to make them want to move forward through your narrative. You'll know you've done your job well if, à la Spillane, you leave them hungry for more.

The way you snare garden visitors is the same way a mystery writer snares readers: by presenting them with something exciting, but at the same time making it clear that there is more. The writer does this by opening with a crime, usually an enigmatic one, and clues that make you believe that if you read on there will be a resolution. The garden designer accomplishes a similar effect by enticing the visitor with a an intriguing entrance—there has to be some immediate payoff—and then layering, interposing screens of some sort, to imply that other things await discovery for the cost of a little time and a few steps.

This sort of tease, incidentally, is especially important in small gardens where an extended exploration isn't really possible. Use layering to partially obscure some back corner, framing it in such a way that it looks like the entrance to a passageway to some other, additional space. With this device, you relieve your postage-stamp garden's sense of constriction.

A garden design also resembles a novel's plot in that, to be effective, the different scenes must connect in a single thread. In the novel, of course, the scenes are connected by the use of the same cast of characters throughout, and by the author's use of the same literary style throughout. In a similar fashion, I often use the same architectural material—a type of stone paving, for example—throughout a garden to relate the different areas to each other. You could achieve the same end by including a characteristic plant in the different areas. Repeating some element of the house (brick paths, for example, with a brick house) is a way to bring the house into the plot. A subtler but very effective way to accomplish this same end is to use the dimensions of the house as the basic unit of measurement in the landscape. In Japan, houses were traditionally designed in multiples of the measurements of the standard tatami, the rice straw mats that, traditionally, were fitted together as floor coverings. Designers of traditional gardens commonly used this same rectangle as the basic unit for laying out a courtyard so that the house and landscape would have a subliminal sense of unity.

One more technique to be learned from the novelist is another use of contrast. A good storyteller varies the mood and pace between chapters to heighten drama and enhance mystery. Lord Voldemort is all staccato dialogue and fast-paced, brutal action; he seems all the more sinister when juxtaposed against Harry Potter's selfless, team-spirited play during a quidditch match or the low comedy of Harry's vacations with Muggle relatives. Similarly, in your garden a shady spot seems cooler and more sheltered if you enter it via an open, sun-baked lawn, and an open, flower-filled meadow is all the more joyously expansive when you emerge into it from the green enclosure of a winding woodland path.

A GARDEN IN NEW YORK STATE

One of the most creative uses of layering I have seen recently was in this garden, which my partner Eric Groft designed for a new home on a generous 25-acre site roughly forty miles from New York City, near the New York–Connecticut border. This was an exceptional opportunity in that Eric and the rest of our firm were involved in the planning process before the construction of the house, so that we were able to work with the architect in determining where within the landscape the house should be set. Jointly, we made the decision to take advantage of a dramatic but challenging spot on a slope by nestling the house between a little knoll and several natural rock outcrops partway down the declivity. By locating the house there, we were able to face its front entrance to the east, where it would catch the morning sun, while opening the back of the house and attached terraces to the a spectacular vista of the sunset over fields, groves, and an existing natural pond.

This created a challenge, however. The topography of the slope and the natural features (knoll and outcrops) that we wanted to preserve limited our options for automobile access to the house. Unless handled carefully, the driveway to the front door and to a service area the client wanted was going to dominate the landscape, turning what should be a rural retreat into a highway bypass. In particular, we didn't want to disrupt the relationship between the front of the house and the knoll.

Eric resolved this by separating the service access from the drive to the front door, running the service access to the north of the house and the front access to the south. He used both natural and constructed features to screen the driveways, and also to layer the garden. These layering devices also served another purpose: that of integrating the house, a striking contemporary structure that had the presence of a piece of abstract sculpture, with its sylvan surroundings.

Thus, the knoll became the focal point for the view from the front of the house, creating an enclosed area into which we inserted an entry garden. The large outcrop on the opposite side of the house, to the west, be-

A HOUSE IN UPSTATE NEW YORK DESIGNED BY ELIZABETH DEMETRIADES.

came a basis for an extensive rock garden. The planting throughout was romantic and informal, an idealized version of the natural fields and woods that stretched away in every direction. We made the steps to the front door out of a granite quarried only a few miles away, in order to link the architecture to the surrounding outcrops. The house, which was otherwise surfaced with zinc-coated copper panels, was clad around the base with a bluestone veneer; we use the same stone to surface the terraces around the house, varying the pattern in which the stone was set to distinguish different areas within the whole.

At the division we wished to make most definite—between the north end of the entry garden and an adjoining dining terrace—Eric set a raised water channel, a sort of bluestone-trimmed concrete trough. This emerges from the grasses and perennials clustered around the foot of the knoll to spill water into a small rectilinear lily pond adjacent to the house

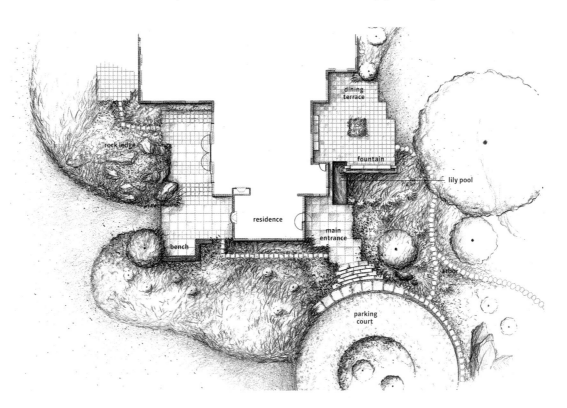

(it's the view from the breakfast nook inside). The artificial rill presents not only a physical barrier but a visual one as well, as the eye is irresistibly drawn to the running water so that in either the entrance garden or the dining terrace, one rarely looks beyond the channel to focus on the other space.

The natural outcrops to the west and more distantly to the east of the house have an enormous innate presence, and by interrupting the landscape and drawing the eye, they, much like the water feature in the entry garden, also function as layering. This type of layering can be very effective; it works in the same way that a magician accomplishes most of his illusions. He draws your glance with some dramatic gesture of one hand so

WOOD BENCH AT LIVING
ROOM TERRACE WITH
THE MEADOW IN THE
BACKGROUND.

OPPOSITE: A MISTY
MORNING REVEALS LAYERS
OF COLOR AND TEXTURE
IN THE VIEW FROM THE
MASTER BEDROOM.

that you don't notice what he is doing with the other one. We didn't rely entirely on prestidigitation, however—we flanked the house with a stone wall that the client, a perfectionist who kept us on our toes, insisted we re-lay perhaps ten times before it met with her approval.

Despite the extent of the landscape, the impression around the house is one of intimacy, of nature rising up in rock and knoll to embrace the habitation. We reinforced this feeling by wrapping the house in layerings of flowering dogwoods and waving masses of grasses and flowers. From the morning, when the sun rises over the knoll to light the rill and lily pond, right through to evening, as the sun fades from view from the westfacing windows and terraces, this is a place set apart in extraordinary peace, a sanctuary in the original and spiritual sense of the word.

A CONVERSATION WITH MARTHA SCHWARTZ

When I get stuck in my work, when I become aware that some aspect of the design I'm developing is, well, boring, I ask myself this question: "What would Martha do?" By Martha I mean, of course, Martha Schwartz.

Martha can be many things—brilliant, glamorous, and bold; outrageous or sensitive and responsive; thoughtful or funny—depending on the circumstances and the occasion. But one thing she never has been, in my experience, is boring.

She emerged on the landscape architecture scene with a bang in 1979. Her then husband and collaborator, Peter Walker (himself a legendary landscape architect), was away on a trip, and Martha decided to transform the front yard of their house in Cambridge, Massachusetts, as a present for his return. So she covered it with purple gravel on which she created a parterre of weatherproofed bagels. Bagels, she noted, are the perfect garden plant: they don't need water and they do well in the shade. After being featured in a cover story in *Landscape Architecture* magazine, Martha moved on to other things. Outraged critics, however, especially those who see gardens only in conventional horticultural terms, are still gobbling with outrage more than thirty years later.

Martha has gone on to design almost every imaginable kind of landscape, from residential gardens to public squares and playgrounds. She's created gardens for a jailhouse in Seattle, a car rental center in Broward County, Florida, and corporate headquarters all around the world, and done many art installations, like the one she created for the Spoleto festival. Through all of this, she has continued to inspire clients with her sleek minimalist design (often characterized by the use of familiar plants in very unfamiliar ways) while functioning as a critical lightning rod. "Hang on to your hollyhocks," warned the British newspaper *The Telegraph* in response to Martha's public charge in 2009 that England had shamefully neglected its public landscape and her suggestions about how the nation could do better.

I like to be challenged, and I see the role of gardens as, at least in part, to change our understanding of our landscape and nature. What's more, a garden without an element of humor strikes me as a poor place. Given these attitudes, I find Martha Schwartz essential and her work a jolt of pure oxygen. Early in the process of creating this book I met Martha at her loft in Cambridge, Massachusetts, to seek her insights. What follows are the high points—her reflections on the factors that have shaped her work.

> My training is in fine art. I grew up always wanting to be an artist. . . . I went to the Philadelphia Museum of Art—they have a program for children. I took classes at the bottom of that museum, which is one of the great museums in the world, really. I just used to wander around there every Saturday morning, looking at stuff, and making art . . . I went to the Philadelphia College of Art when I was in high school.
>
> —
>
> I was primarily involved in two-dimensional stuff, not three-dimensional stuff, not sculpture. . . . And then I went to the

University of Michigan School of Fine Arts . . . and really focused on printmaking. But during that time, that was also the time when the Earthworks artists were coming on board. I was really turned on and intrigued and in love with that stuff. With Robert Smithson and his *Spiral Jetty*. Michael Heizer's work, Walter de Maria, Nancy Holt's Sun Tunnels. These were amazing works of art. Not just physically—physically they were beautiful, but they were works of art that were out there in the landscape and they were *about* the landscape, but there was some kind of dialogue between the pieces and the site . . . they were really bellwethers of the environmental movement. . . . I decided I did want to learn how to build big art. That's why I'm a landscape architect.

—

I'm always interested in what sort of art [my clients are] into. Always. You can really see deeply into someone when you take a look at the art [they own].

—

You know, I've seen all sorts of collections. You're going to have people who have [pieces by] the very best artists, but not very good pieces of the best artists. They know who the [best] are, but they can't see very well. Or you have people who collect [artists] who are not particularly well known, but they have great pieces because they're doing it on a very personal basis.

—

I tend to value contemporary art most of all. Because it's a reflection of who we are today. It's about taking your pulse, taking your temperature. How are you feeling today? What are the things that are on your mind? What's bothering you and what just really turns you on?

—

I look at art all the time. I love to go look at art. Because when I'm looking at art, I'm actually looking for ideas. Landscape ideas. You can see them in paintings, you can see them in installations, you can see them in sculpture, you can hear it in music, you can hear it in a play. There are things that strike you about just being a human being and about how people live, what people want, what they yearn for, what beauty is, that can help to inspire you.

—

Well, I don't think a garden is fundamentally about plants. . . . A garden is primarily about mental space . . . I think it's about a place that people go to get away from everything else. To get away from their everyday world, to get away from whatever is bothering them. To get away from the pressures of day-to-day life and to somehow take time to connect to something greater. Maybe that's nature, or maybe that's God, or maybe that's their inner selves, or maybe it's Buddha. Or maybe it's . . . whatever. But it's some other place that you can take refuge in and exist on another plane. That for me is a garden. I think that the plants are in service to creating that mental space.

—

You have to decide what is your mental space. It's very personal. Is your mental space a white box with the sky above it, where it's absolutely disembodied and you're floating? Is your space something that's about an openness? Is it about closure?

Is it about color? Does that take you there? What do you want it to be? Then you get the plants and you get the materials, and you make form so you can create this wonderful place.

—

We build our environment and our environment shapes us.

EPILOGUE

WHAT THIS BOOK HAS DESCRIBED is not a method but rather a voyage of discovery—if, as a gardener and designer, you set off down this road, you'll find it never ends. You won't want it to end—my own experience has been that the trip is wonderful in itself. Not only will your experiences with music and the other arts enhance your gardening, but what you accomplish with trowel and spade will enrich the pleasure you find in other arts.

As children we experiment unself-consciously with paints and clay and blocks. Somewhere along the line, though, most of us become convinced that we don't have the necessary "talent" to pursue the arts, and we stop expressing our dreams in this fashion. We fall mute.

I believe, though, the obstacle almost always isn't a lack of talent. The problem is that you (like so many others) didn't find the proper medium in which to express yourself. If you love working in the soil as much as I do, if you find foliages, barks, and flowers as fascinating as I do, then perhaps the true medium for your self-expression is in the landscape. Maybe it is because the materials with which we work in gardening are alive, beings in their own right, that the process of arranging and ordering them feels like a collaboration rather than a solo performance. In any case, I find that working out-of-doors in the garden is entirely free of the sort of self-consciousness and stage fright that can make other types of artistic creation so intimidating.

Take up your trowel and spade, then, and turn your dreams loose. As you explore and shape those dreams, I believe you'll come to understand better and better the work of your fellow artists, the ones who chose other media. Paying attention to what they teach will transform your garden. It can also return you to a childlike openness to all those other arts you set aside. Who can say which gift is the greater?

ACKNOWLEDGMENTS

I would like to acknowledge my partners Lisa Delplace, Eric Groft, and Sheila Brady for their contribution and collaboration on the projects included in this book. They are now leading the firm, and without them none of this would be possible.

I would also like to acknowledge my partner of thirty-five years, Wolfgang Oehme.

The enthusiasm and energy of my editor, David Ebershoff, contributed invaluable clarity to the concept and text. Barbara Bachman, part of his team and the book's designer, has given it great beauty.

My literary agent, Helen Pratt, introduced me to Random House, for which I am eternally grateful.

Tom Christopher was a joy to work with on the text and we had a lot of fun traveling together to see the gardens and do the interviews. Tom captures my voice perfectly.

I'm greatly indebted to Steel Colony for his attention to details and sage advice.

Marisa Scalera produced the exquisite drawings, each of which stands alone as a work of art.

Vernae Jones-Seals kept accurate accounts. Charles and Martha Turner were watchdogs for accurate text.

Finally, I wish to thank the clients who made these gardens possible through their commitment to beauty and courage to innovate. I'm grateful to them for allowing us to revisit and photograph their gardens.

—James van Sweden

It has been a great privilege (and pleasure) to work with James van Sweden and all his talented colleagues at Oehme, van Sweden & Associates.

I also owe a debt of gratitude to all the artists who took the time out from their busy schedules to talk with us about their endeavors in various media.

Finally, I want to thank Ruth Clausen, an extraordinary horticulturist and an even better friend. For thirty-five years she has provided answers, inspiration, and support—without her coaxing and encouragement, this book would never have been finished.

—Tom Christopher

CREDITS

PHOTOGRAPHERS

James van Sweden *unless otherwise noted*

ILLUSTRATORS

ABOUT THE AUTHORS

Following training as an architect and landscape architect in the United States and the Netherlands, JAMES VAN SWEDEN formed a partnership with landscape architect and horticulturist Wolfgang Oehme. A revolutionary garden style quickly emerged and continues to flourish today at their international firm, Oehme, van Sweden & Associates. Van Sweden's first book, *Bold Romantic Gardens*, co-authored with Oehme, is considered a classic in the field. James van Sweden is a Fellow of the American Society of Landscape Architects and the recipient of many awards, including the prestigious 2010 ASLA Design Medal, the top honor in the field of landscape architecture. He lives in Washington, D.C.

After completing a degree in classics at Brown University, TOM CHRISTOPHER returned to his roots: he resumed his life-long interest in gardening and apprenticed for two years at the New York Botanical Garden. Subsequent to graduation from NYBG's School of Professional Horticulture, he spent a decade restoring the landscape of a historic Hudson River Valley estate. He has written articles for *The New York Times* and served as a columnist at *House & Garden* and *Martha Stewart Living*. The author of seven books, he currently gardens in the hills of western Massachusetts.